ECONOMIC AND SOCIAL COMMISSION FOR ASIA AND THE PACIFIC

STATISTICAL PROFILES   No. 15

WOMEN IN THE ISLAMIC REPUBLIC OF IRAN

A COUNTRY PROFILE

UNITED NATIONS
New York, 1998

ST/ESCAP/1768

UNITED NATIONS PUBLICATION
Sales No. E.98.II.F.64
Copyright © United Nations 1998
ISBN: 92-1-119851-8

The views expressed in this profile are those of the author and do not necessarily reflect those of the United Nations. The designations employed and the presentation of the material in this publication do not imply the expression of any opinion whatsoever on the part of the Secretariat of the United Nations concerning the legal status of any country, territory, city or area, or of its authorities, or concerning the delimitation of its frontiers or boundaries. Mention of firm names and commercial products does not imply the endorsement of the United Nations.

The profile has been prepared under project BK-X20-3-214, on improving statistics on women in the ESCAP region.

FOREWORD

The call for the development of statistics and indicators on the situation of women has, for some time, been voiced in various global and regional forums. It was first recommended by the World Plan of Action for the Implementation of the Objectives of the International Women's Year, adopted in 1975. The recommendations of the World Plan of Action were reaffirmed and elaborated in the Programme of Action for the Second Half of the United Nations Decade for Women: Equality, Development and Peace. On various occasions, the Commission, stressing the importance of social and human development, has recognized the need for improved statistics and indicators on women. It has noted that better indicators are required to monitor the situation of women and to assess the effectiveness of strategies and programmes designed to address priority gender issues.

The secretariat initiated the project on improving statistics on women in the ESCAP region in 1994. The project aims to support governments in their efforts to promote the full integration of women in development and improve their status in line with the Nairobi Forward-looking Strategies for the Advancement of Women adopted in 1985. The project has been implemented by the Economic and Social Commission for Asia and the Pacific (ESCAP) through its subprogramme on statistics, with funding assistance from the Government of the Netherlands.

As a major component of its activities, the project commissioned experts from 19 countries in the region to prepare country profiles on the situation of women and men in the family, at work, and in public life, by analysing available statistical data and information. The profiles are intended to highlight the areas where action is needed, and to raise the consciousness of readers about issues concerning women and men. The 19 countries are Bangladesh, China, India, Indonesia, the Islamic Republic of Iran, Japan, Nepal, Pakistan, the Philippines, the Republic of Korea, Sri Lanka and Thailand in Asia; and Cook Islands, Fiji, Papua New Guinea, Samoa, Solomon Islands, Tonga and Vanuatu in the Pacific.

The secretariat hosted two meetings each in Asia and in the Pacific as part of the project activities. At the first meeting, the experts discussed and agreed on the structure, format and contents of the country profiles, based on guidelines prepared by the secretariat through Ms C.N. Ericta, consultant. The second meeting was a workshop to review the draft profiles. Participants in the workshop included the country experts and invited representatives from national statistical offices of Brunei Darussalam, Hong Kong, China, the Lao People's Democratic Republic, Mongolia and Viet Nam in Asia; of Marshall Islands, Tuvalu, and Vanuatu in the Pacific; and representatives of United Nations organizations, specialized agencies and international organizations.

The original draft of the present profile, *Women in the Islamic Republic of Iran*, was prepared by Ms Mehrangiz Changizi Ashtiani, Researcher in Manpower Statistics, Statistical Centre of Iran. It was technically edited and modified by the ESCAP secretariat with the assistance of Mr S. Selvaratnam, consultant. The profiles express the views of the authors and not necessarily those of the secretariat.

I wish to express my sincere appreciation to the Government of the Netherlands for its generous financial support, which enabled the secretariat to implement the project.

Adrianus Mooy
Executive Secretary

iii

CONTENTS

LIST OF TABLES

LIST OF TABLES *(continued)*

LIST OF ANNEX TABLES

PART I

DESCRIPTIVE ANALYSIS

INTRODUCTION

The Constitution of the Islamic Republic of Iran, while emphasizing the vital role and obligations of women as mothers and wives, also stresses the importance of supporting women's rights and of creating an environment conducive to securing women's development and progress in all spheres. The Islamic government has also committed itself to the provision of all necessary means, including appropriate legislation, to enhance women's educational, scientific, social and political capacity so as to enable them to fully participate in and benefit from overall national development.

In pursuance of the stated policies and goals, the government has, among other things, created the necessary institutions to address issues related to women. The first concrete action in this regard was the establishment in June 1987 of a high-level Women's Social and Cultural Council (WSCC) under a mandate by the Supreme Council of the Cultural Revolution. WSCC, which comprises representatives of women's organizations, the Supreme Council, ministries of education, culture, health, labour and interior, as well as revolutionary institutions and scholars, is responsible for the formulation of policy guidelines on the social and cultural needs of women and for the creation of a suitable environment for their personal and spiritual development. Since its inception, WSCC has prepared and submitted for the approval of the Supreme Council several draft bills and proposals, including those on the mandatory setting up of nursery schools for children of working mothers, and the creation of civil courts for family assistance and guidance. WSCC has also forwarded several policy suggestions and sectoral issues on women in development for incorporation in the national development plans.

In 1991, on the recommendations of WSCC, the President of the Islamic Republic appointed the first Adviser to the President on Women's Affairs, and also created a high-level organization, the Bureau of Women's Affairs, as an umbrella organization for women's activities in the country. The Bureau, located in the President's Office and headed by the Adviser, has as its mandatory functions the coordination of various women's activities and the promotion of women's socio-economic status. It functions as a catalyst, rather than as an administrative and implementing agency, in familiarizing women with their human and Islamic rights and facilitating women's access to their legal entitlements in various cultural, social, economic and other spheres. The Bureau performs its mandated functions through three departments or sections: Planning and Research, Domestic Relations, and International Cooperation.

With the assistance and support of all development-oriented ministries, the Bureau has established women-in-development focal points or women's units in each ministry to mainstream women's issues into the policies and programmes of the respective ministries. More specifically, the focal points are expected to maintain communication with all women officials of their respective ministries to gather information on activities relating to women in development undertaken by the ministries; to identify talented women from within the ministry and make use of them for programmes related to women in development; to design, develop and propose projects consistent with the mandate of their own ministry for submission to the Bureau; to ensure that themes related to women in development are reflected in the plan of action of each ministry; and to help establish liaison between various professional associations under each ministry and the Bureau. At present, women's units are well established in all ministries and government institutions.

The government has also created the Women's Affairs Commission, with its central office in the Ministry of Interior. At the provincial level, women's commissions have been set up in the Social Councils of various provinces to facilitate the advancement of women, to identify their problems and to promote their participation in social and political activities. The main functions of the Commission and its provincial network are (a) to undertake a systematic survey of family conditions and of the legal, educational and economic status of women in order to identify problems hindering the advancement of women; (b) to collect statistics and other information on different aspects of women's lives and activities; and (c) to create facilities to .encourage women's participation in cultural, social, economic and artistic endeavours.

The number of non-governmental organizations (NGOs) engaged in activities related to the welfare of women has increased substantially since the Islamic Revolution owing to the availability of appropriate government support for the formation and registration of such organizations. The NGOs, which were initially stimulated by revolutionary fervour and nurtured by popular support and religious beliefs, had gradually matured during the war with Iraq and developed into successful organizations. A leading women's NGO is the Islamic Women's Institute, founded in 1978, which has as its main goals the improvement of the status of Iranian women through training in income-generating activities; increasing awareness among women about their social and economic situation; and helping them by establishing cooperatives. The Institute also conducts research on women's issues and publishes magazines, booklets and other information materials.

As a result of the initiative taken by the government as well as the NGOs, existing laws and regulations have been reviewed and where necessary suitable amendments made to remove provisions and practices that discriminated against women. Further, new laws have been enacted or additional provisions made to existing laws to grant women the same rights and entitlements as men in such matters as marriage, divorce and employment.

On account of the various measures adopted and programmes implemented, considerable progress has been made since the 1970s in enhancing the status of Iranian women in various aspects of life. For instance, the health of women and children has improved remarkably and this is reflected in substantial declines in the respective mortality rates and an increase in life expectancy. Iranian women have also rapidly overcome the constraints which have in the past hindered their education, and over the years an increasing number of girls have been entering the education system at all levels, more have stayed longer in the system, and more have obtained basic educational qualifications. There has also been an increase in the number of women seeking employment outside the home, and a specific trend in women's employment has been their increasing preference for professional jobs. The representation of women in decision-making positions in the legislative and executive branches has also improved during the past two decades.

Despite these achievements, Iranian women still lag behind their male counterparts in regard to their role and status in many areas. Educational enrolments, particularly at secondary and tertiary levels, continue to be in favour of males, and the illiteracy rate is considerably higher among females than males. Maternal mortality rates are still high in comparison with countries with similar income levels. The labour-force participation rate of Iranian women is among the lowest in the world. Only a very small proportion of the political office-holders and senior-level decision-making government executives are women. There are also marked differences in these indicators between urban and rural areas.

The Islamic Republic of Iran has yet to formulate a comprehensive policy on women as well as a long-term plan with specific goals and targets for the development of the country's women. The drawing-up of such policies and plans will require, *inter alia,* up-to-date and accurate data and information on the current situation of women vis-à-vis men in various areas of concern. Fortunately, the national machinery for this purpose is already in place and several institutions, such as the Statistical Centre of Iran and various ministries, collect and process relevant statistical data and information on a continuing basis. It is, however, very important to bring together the available data and information in a coordinated and systematic manner so as to ascertain the nature and adequacy of the available statistical information and the additional information that needs to be collected and analysed to obtain a more comprehensive picture of the situation of women in the country.

The present profile attempts to bring together the available data and information on the country's women, as well as to highlight the gaps in the existing database. It is hoped that, with suitable modifications, it can be used as a model for the systematic collection and analysis of data and information relevant to women's issues.

A. HIGHLIGHTS

The setting

1. The Islamic Republic of Iran has a highly diverse topography and climate. A series of massive heavily eroded mountain ranges surround the high interior basin. The climate is complex, ranging from sub-tropical to sub-polar. The total land area is 636,296 square miles, or 1,648 thousand square kilometres.

2. The Constitution provides for a Vali-ye Faqih (religious leader) who carries the burden of leadership and is above the Constitution. Legislative power is vested in the 270-member Majlis, and the chief executive of the administration is the President. A 12-member Council of Guardians supervises elections and ensures that legislation is in accordance with the Constitution and with Islamic precepts.

3. For convenience of administration, the country is divided into 24 provinces, 229 counties, 604 districts, 2,103 villages and 514 cities.

4. In 1995, the population was estimated to be 68.4 million and growing at a rate of less than 2 per cent per annum. The population is very unevenly distributed, with the main concentrations being in Azarbayejan, the Caspian region, the watered mountain valleys and the oases. Nearly 57 per cent of the population live in urban areas. Tehran, the capital, is the largest city in the country, with an enumerated population of 6.5 million in 1991.

5. The Islamic Republic of Iran is a multilingual and multi-religious country. However,

Farsi or Persian is the language spoken by the majority of the people and is the official language. Islam, the religion practised by 99 per cent of the people, is the state religion.

6. With a per capita income estimated at US$ 2,200 in 1992, the Islamic Republic of Iran belongs to the group of low-middle income countries. Although it is a major oil-exporting country, its economy is largely agrarian. However, substantial progress has been made over the years in diversifying the sources of national income.

7. The government has developed a national education system providing compulsory education at the primary level and expanding facilities for secondary and tertiary education. The current system provides for separate facilities for the education of boys and girls and places emphasis on agricultural and vocational education programmes.

8. The health services, which were rather rudimentary during the first half of this century, have been improved considerably since then with the development of a network of health-care facilities, including large hospitals, nursing homes, health houses and health centres throughout the country. Special attention has been paid to the needs of women and children in the provision of health facilities.

Women's profile

1. In the Islamic Republic of Iran, males have outnumbered females in all census enumerations, and in 1991 there were about 106 males per 100 females, or 94 females for every 100 males.

2. The high fertility which had existed in the country until recent years has resulted in an age structure in which children and youth under 20 years of age constitute about 35 per cent of the total population.

3. Among persons aged 10 years and over, about 56 per cent of females as against 52 per cent of males were reported to be married in 1991. The proportion widowed among females (5.9 per cent) was over four times that among males (1.4 per cent).

4. Since 1976/77, there has been a dramatic increase in educational enrolments and this increase has been more marked for females than for males. In 1993/94, females constituted 47.2 per cent of total enrolments at the primary level, 43.3 per cent at junior secondary level, and 45.4 per cent at senior secondary level. However, women are very much under-represented in institutions of higher education, constituting about 30 per cent of total enrolments in all universities in 1993/94.

5. The literacy rate of persons aged six years and over has been increasing rapidly since 1976, this increase being more pronounced for females than for males. Yet, in 1991, the female literacy rate of 67.4 per cent was 13.2 percentage points lower than the male rate.

6. With increasing attention being paid to the health of women and mothers, the maternal mortality rate is estimated to have declined rapidly over the years. There have also been dramatic reductions in infant and child mortality rates in recent decades.

7. Since the second half of this century, there have been remarkable improvements in life expectancy at birth for males as well as females, and in 1990-1995 females had an estimated life expectancy of 68.0 years, or one year longer than the 67.0 years estimated for males.

Women in family life

1. Modernization and urbanization have resulted in the gradual replacement of the traditional extended family system by the nuclear family as the basic social unit. This transformation is also enabling women to play an increasingly important role in decision-making and management of family matters.

2. In 1991, about 6 per cent of all households in the country were headed by females. The majority of the female household heads were aged 50 years and over and were also illiterate.

3. In recent decades there have been significant changes in marriage customs and patterns, with a decrease in the incidence of consanguineous marriages, children having a greater say in the choice of their marriage partners, and an increasing tendency among young persons to delay their marriage, as reflected in the rising average age at first marriage and the decreasing proportion of ever-married at prime marriageable ages.

4. Recent decades have also witnessed remarkable changes in the reproductive patterns and behaviour of married couples. The average number of children born to a woman during her reproductive life is today almost half what it was 20 years ago. Country-wide surveys also point to a considerable increase in the knowledge about and practice of contraception among married women in the country.

5. With the enactment of laws to curb men's rights to arbitrary divorce and granting women rights to seek divorce if deemed necessary, there has been a significant decrease in the incidence of divorce. In 1991, less than 0.5 per cent of males as well as females aged 10 years and over were reported to be divorced.

Women in economic life

1. Despite constitutional provisions and legal enactments supporting women's employment, the labour-force participation rate of Iranian women is not only considerably lower than that of their male counterparts but is also among the lowest in the world.

2. The proportion of the labour force that is reported to be employed is also comparatively lower among females compared with males; in 1991, about 25 per cent of the economically active females were unemployed, the corresponding proportion among males being only 9.5 per cent.

3. In 1991, nearly 50 per cent of the employed females were engaged in the service sector while another about 25 per cent were employed in the manufacturing sector. The proportion of employed females in the agricultural sector decreased markedly, from 26.6 per cent in 1986 to 12.9 per cent in 1991.

4. Although the proportion of employed females in professional and technical occupations had

increased substantially over the years, the majority of females in this occupational category are engaged in jobs that are relatively low-paid and carry a low status.

5. Nearly 60 per cent of employed females compared with 50 per cent among employed males are wage or salaried workers, and about 50 per cent of the employed females are in the public sector.

Women in public life

1. Iranian women played a prominent role in political and public affairs during the cultural revolution of the 1970s and during the war with Iraq in the 1980s. Since then, women have been active in various aspects of national political processes.

2. Although an increasing number of women have been nominated as candidates and an increasing percentage of eligible women have voted at elections, women are very much under-represented in the national legislative bodies.

3. The number of women recruited to the public service has been increasing rapidly over the years. While women constitute about a third of all public sector employees, they occupy less than 5 per cent of decision-making and management-level positions.

4. Several occupations explicitly restrict the employment of women; they are not appointed to the judiciary and are not recruited to the armed services.

B. THE SETTING

1. Location and physical features

The Islamic Republic of Iran, known as Persia until 1935, is situated in Western Asia between 25° and 45° north latitude and 44° and 63° east longitude. It is bounded to the north by Azerbaijan and Turkmenistan, to the west by Turkey and Iraq, to the south by the Persian Gulf and the Gulf of Oman, and to the east by Pakistan and Afghanistan. It also controls about a dozen islands in the Persian Gulf.

The total land area of the country is 636,296 square miles, or about 1,648 thousand square kilometres. More than 30 per cent of its 4,865-mile boundary is sea coast.

In terms of topography and climate, it is a highly diverse country. There are two main topographical features: a mountainous rim on all four sides; and the central plateau. The mountainous rim consists of the Zagros mountain chain on the north-west, west and south, with numerous peaks rising to 8,000 feet, a few of them between 10,000 and 13,000 feet; the Elburz mountain chain, which runs along the south shore of the Caspian to meet the border ranges of Khorasan to the east; and less massive and more intermittent mountains on the east.

The heartland lies in the central plateau, much of which is salt and sand desert, including both the Dasht-e Kavir and Dasht-e Lut systems. Fertile areas abound where water resources are adequate to support irrigated agriculture, such as the Esfahan basin, northern Khorasan, and the Qazvin and Varamin plains. Only about 11 per cent of the total land area is under cultivation, while another 27 per cent is under permanent pasture and meadowland. Forests and woodland constitute another 11 per cent of the total land area (table 1). There are three large rivers, but only one – the Kharun – is navigable. The other two, the Atrak and Safid systems, are too steep and irregular.

Table 1. Land-use pattern: 1992

Land-use type	Area (thousand ha)	Percentage of total
Land under cultivation	18 170	11.1
Arable land	*16 650*	*10.2*
Permanent crops	*1 520*	*0.9*
Permanent pasture and meadowland	44 000	26.9
Forest and woodland	18 020	11.0
Other	83 410	51.0
Total land area	163 600	100.0

Source: The Economist Intelligence Unit, *Country Profile: Iran, 1996/97.*

The climate is one of great extremes, with very hot and dry summers when temperatures soar to nearly 50°C (131°F), and cold winters with temperatures dipping to a low of 18°C or 0°F or below. Temperatures also vary from a high of 51°C or 123°F in Khugestan at the head of the Persian Gulf to a low of − 37°C or 35°F in Azarbayejan in the north-west. More than one third of the land surface receives rainfall on an average of more than 250 mm annually. Winter is normally the rainy season for the country as a whole.

2. Government and administration

Since 1906 and until 1979, the Islamic Republic of Iran was a constitutional monarchy with a parliamentary system of government. The Majlis, or legislature, consisted of 120 members elected for a two-year term, and the Shah could nominate half the members of the 60-member upper house. The judiciary was divided into civil and religious courts, and Shia Islam was declared the official religion.

But the 1979 revolution ushered in an Islamic Constitution according to which all branches of the government – legislative, executive, and judiciary – are governed by the Islamic laws under the supervision of the Vali-ye faqih, the Supreme Imam. Article 110 of the Constitution gave the person who held the office of the Vali-ye-faqih sweeping powers, including the right to appoint the highest judicial authorities, to judge the suitability of presidential candidates and to be commander-in-chief. The second highest official in the new republic was the President, who was directly elected by the people and was responsible for nominating the Prime Minister, who in turn nominated the Cabinet with the approval of the President. The 1979 Constitution created a new Majlis of 270 members elected by universal suffrage for a four-year term.

The 1989 amendment to the Constitution abolished the post of Prime Minister. In the current structure, the Imam, as the religious leader, is considered above the Constitution. The President, directly elected by the people, is responsible for implementing and safeguarding constitutional provisions and coordinating all three branches of government. He is also the head of the executive branch and presides over the Cabinet. The executive branch is responsible for the country's overall socio-economic development.

The legislative branch is composed of the Parliament (Majlis), the highest legislative body of the government consisting of 270 popularly elected members; the Council of Guardians, consisting of 12 jurists and lawyers and responsible for ensuring that all laws passed by the Majlis are in conformity with Islamic tenets and principles; and the Expediency Council of 22 members, to which any dispute between the Majlis and the Council of Guardians is referred for arbitration and final approval. The judiciary, responsible for the dispensation of justice, comprises the Supreme Court, lower civil and criminal courts, and a special civil court. The Administrative Justice Tribunal arbitrates matters related to the violation of rules and regulations by governmental organizations.

For administrative purposes, the country is divided into 24 provinces (*ostans*), 229 counties (*shahrestans*), 604 districts (*bakhshs*), 2,103 villages (*dehestans*) and 514 cities.

3. Population growth and distribution

The population of the Islamic Republic of Iran, estimated at 9.9 million at the beginning of this century, had slowly increased to 18.9 million in 1956 when the first modern census was taken in the country. Since then the population has grown rapidly, reaching 34.3 million at the 1976 census, 49.4 million in 1986 and 55.8 million in 1991 (table 2). In other words, while it had taken more than half a century, from 1900 to 1956, for the country's population to double itself, a trebling of the population had occurred in a matter of 35 years between 1956 and 1991. In view of the suspected under-enumeration, the population is considered to be higher than that reported by the censuses. Recent estimates prepared by the United Nations Secretariat place the population at 59.2 million in 1990 and at 68.4 million in 1995.

According to various estimates, the population growth rate, which averaged less than 1.0 per cent a year during the first quarter of this

Table 2. Estimated and enumerated population, and average annual growth rate of population: 1900-1991

Year	Population (millions)	Average annual growth rate (percentage)
1900	9.9[a]	–
1927	12.0[a]	0.8
1935	13.5[a]	1.5
1941	14.8[a]	1.5
1956	18.9[b]	2.2
1966	25.7[b]	3.1
1976	33.7[b]	2.7
1986	49.4[b]	3.8
1991	55.8[b]	2.5

Source: Akbar Aghajanian, "A new direction in population policy and family planning in the Islamic Republic of Iran", *Asia-Pacific Population Journal*, vol. 10, No. 1 (1995).

[a] Estimated.
[b] Enumerated.

century, almost doubled to 1.5 per cent during the second quarter, reflecting improvements in the standards of living of the people. But since the Second World War there was a further acceleration in this rate to 3.1 per cent between 1956 and 1966 owing to the substantial decline in mortality, while fertility remained almost unchanged at traditionally high levels. However, with a decline in fertility, the annual rate of growth decreased to 2.7 per cent between 1966 and 1976, but rose again to an all-time high of 3.8 per cent between 1976 and 1986, owing largely to an influx of refugees from neighbouring countries, especially Afghanistan. There was a decline in the rate of growth of the population to 2.5 per cent during the period 1986-1991 and to less than 2.0 per cent in 1995.

The population is also unevenly distributed, with more than 78 per cent concentrated in the western regions and the remaining 22 per cent spread out in the northern and eastern regions. The distribution of the population tends to be correlated with the ability of the land to support it, with a density of over 100 persons per km² in well-watered territories along the Caspian coast and east Azarbayejan, but ranging from as low as 5 in Semnan Province to 17 in Khorasan Province.

The population distribution is also characterized by concentration in urban areas because of the continuing high rates of internal growth as well as the steady influx of migrants from rural areas, possibly in search of employment. By and large, the rural population has grown more slowly, while urban areas experienced a rapid increase of more than 4 per cent a year. Data from the censuses indicate that the proportion of the total population residing in urban areas increased from about 31 per cent in the 1950s to 57 per cent in 1991. According to the 1991 census, 42.3 per cent of the population lived in rural areas while the remaining 0.7 per cent were nomads and settled tribes. The largest urban agglomeration is Tehran, with a population of 6,475,527 in 1991.

4. Language and religion

The Islamic Republic of Iran is a multi-lingual and diverse cultural society. Farsi, the Persian language proper, is spoken by over 50 per cent of the population as their first language, while Turkish-speaking Iranians account for about 22 per cent of the population. These are descendants of Aryan tribes, whose origins are lost in antiquity. The Kurds, a fierce nomadic people living in the western mountains, and constituting about 5.5 per cent of the population, speak Kurdish, while a group of semi-nomadic people, constituting about 6 per cent of the total population, speak Luri, a Persian dialect. In addition, Baluchi, Arabic, Armenian and Assyrian, spoken by small minorities, are regionally important. However, Farsi, which is the official language and also operates as a lingua franca for minority groups, is spoken by an estimated 83 per cent of the people throughout the country – 91 per cent in urban and 73 per cent in rural areas.

The vast majority of Iranians (99 per cent) are Muslims, and Islam is the state religion. The great majority of the Persians and Azarbayejanis are Shia Muslims and account for 91 per cent of the country's population. Sunni Muslims, who account for about 8 per cent of the population, are to be largely found among the Kurds in the north-west and Baluchi tribes in the south-east. Major religious minorities include Christians (former Armenians), Jews and Zoroastrians.

The Islamic Republic of Iran also has a substantial refugee population which, according to various estimates, numbers between 2.4 and 4.5 million; more than 80 per cent are from Afghanistan.

5. The economy

The Islamic Republic of Iran is a lower-middle income country with a per capita gross national product (GNP) estimated at US$ 2,200 in 1992. National income estimates prepared for the first time in 1959 indicate that gross domestic product (GDP) then amounted to US$ 3.69 billion, with agriculture contributing 27 per cent and oil a mere 11 per cent.

Available estimates also show that there have been considerable fluctuations in the annual rate of economic growth during the past three decades. After stagnation in the early 1960s, the economy experienced sustained expansion between 1964 and 1973. During this nine-year period, the annual growth rate accelerated from an average of 9.5 per cent between 1962 and 1968 to 11.8 per cent during the period 1968-1973, as oil became a leading sector. However, the growth rate declined sharply to 6.9 per cent between 1973 and 1978 owing to the poor performance of the oil industry. During the period 1980-1985, GDP grew at an average rat of 8 per cent, but dropped to 3 per cent during the period 1985-1989 owing, among other factors, to intense fighting with Iraq and a drop in oil prices. After 1989, however, the rate of growth began to rise, averaging 7.3 per cent during the period 1989-1993.

Agriculture, including forestry and fishing, continues to be the leading sector, accounting for 21.5 per cent of GDP in 1994/95 (table 3) and employing about 25 per cent of the country's labour force in 1994. The principal cash crops are fresh and dried fruits, which accounted for about 13 per cent of non-petroleum earnings in 1994/95. By far the largest acreage is devoted to cereal crops, mainly wheat, barley and paddy rice, followed by cotton and sugar beet. Production of mutton and lamb, beef and veal, and of poultry meat is also important. Fishing is also important, and fish are caught for both domestic consumption and export. More than 200 species

Table 3. Percentage distribution of gross domestic product by sectoral origin: 1991/92 to 1994/95

Major sector	1991/92	1992/93	1993/94	1994/95
Agriculture, forestry and fishing	23.1	23.9	20.8	21.5
Oil	8.2	9.1	17.6	18.6
Mining	0.5	0.5	0.5	0.5
Manufacturing	14.0	14.3	13.7	13.6
Electricity, gas and water	1.1	1.3	1.2	1.0
Construction	4.4	4.0	3.3	3.2
Trade, restaurant and hotel	17.8	17.6	15.5	15.4
Transport, storage and communications	9.0	8.2	7.0	6.2
Financial, real estate and business services	11.0	10.6	9.3	8.4
Other services	10.9	10.5	11.1	11.8
Total	100.0	100.0	100.0	100.0

Source: Bank Markaz Iran, annual reports cited in Economist Intelligence Unit, *Country Profile: Iran, 1996/97.*

of fish are found in the Persian Gulf, of which 150 are edible.

Industry (including oil, mining, manufacturing, construction and power) contributed an estimated 36.9 per cent of GDP in 1994/95 and employed 27.6 per cent of the working population in 1991. Oil occupies a central position in the national economy, its contribution to GDP having more than doubled from 8.2 per cent in 1991/92 to 18.6 per cent in 1994/95. The Islamic Republic of Iran accounts for about 10 per cent of the world's total recoverable oil reserves. Manufacturing accounted for 13.6 per cent of GDP in 1994/95. Traditional handicraft goods, including high-grade silk and cotton carpets, remain important.

Despite the impressive overall economic performance at the national level, the distribution of income at household and regional levels is skewed. A 1989 survey showed that 40 per cent of low-income families shared only 14 per cent of the total income, whereas 20 per cent of the high-income families accounted for 48.5 per cent of the total income. Studies also show that 212 of the 586 districts, representing 20 per cent of the total population, are deprived of basic social facilities. In 1992, the average annual income of an urban household (3,541,277 rials) was nearly twice that of a rural household (1,973,838 rials).

6. Social infrastructure

(a) Education

Traditionally, education outside urban centres concentrated on oral poetic and narrative teachings and oral Islamic instructions. The first advance towards more widespread literacy was made in the years leading up to the Second World War. However, a coordinated push to improve the situation was not made until the 1960s, when the central government launched a mass campaign under the Literacy Programme. A literacy corps was established in 1962 consisting of educated armed services draftees who were sent as teachers into the villages. The education system was changed after the revolution to ensure that all teachings conformed to enunciated Islamic principles.

In terms of the current system of education, primary education, which is provided free, starts at age six and lasts for five years. Although primary education is officially compulsory, this has not been strictly implemented in rural areas. According to the data published by the United Nations Educational, Scientific and Cultural Organization (UNESCO), there were 61,323 primary schools in the country with a total pupil enrolment of 9,937,369 in 1992. Secondary education begins at age 11 and lasts up to seven years, with a first cycle of three years and a second cycle of four years. Total enrolment in general secondary education amounted to 5,995,051 in 1992 (table 4).

After the revolution, the universities were closed for a long period, reopening in 1983 with modified Islamic syllabuses and controlled intake of "acceptable" students. There were 636,254 students enrolled at the universities and equivalent institutions in 1991.

Post-revolution policy has been to eliminate mixed schools; the current system separates boys and girls in school at the age of seven.

Table 4. Number of educational institutions, teachers and students by level of education: 1992

Level of education	Institutions	Teachers	Students
Pre-primary	3 003	6 885	168 864
Primary	61 323	311 839	9 937 369
Secondary			
General	..	211 711	5 995 051
Teacher-training	..	1 590	48 256
Vocational	..	19 457	279 681
Higher[a]			
Universities etc.	..	19 564	256 212
Distance learning	..	1 691	339 272
Others	..	3 953	40 770

Source: United Nations Educational, Scientific and Cultural Organization, *Statistical Yearbook, 1996.*

[a] Referring to 1991.
Two dots (..) indicate that data are not available.

Female teachers are assigned to girls' schools and male teachers to boys' schools. Married women are not permitted to continue in the same school along with unmarried girls. Greater emphasis has been placed on agricultural and vocational programmes, with a reduction in instruction in art and music. The policy also stipulates that vocational guidance should take into account the kind of occupations needed by women, which could be best fulfilled by them, and which are most appropriate for their role and responsibility in the family.

(b) Health and sanitation

Available evidence indicates that despite considerable investment in the health sector during the Shah's regime, the country's health facilities and services had remained far from adequate until the second half of this century. Most of the available facilities and personnel were concentrated in Tehran and other large urban centres, and were hardly accessible to the vast majority of the people residing in the rural and remote areas. The situation was further exacerbated by the shortage of medical personnel and low quality of medical auxiliaries. Consequently, the improvement in the health status of the people was slow in comparison with the improved levels of wealth generated by oil income.

After the revolution, there were further setbacks resulting from the exodus to foreign countries of a large number of highly qualified doctors and other medical personnel. This situation was only partly offset by the return to the country of those doctors exiled under the previous regime or dedicated to the Islamic cause. The development of the health sector was also considerably hampered by the war with Iraq. However, the quality and accessibility of the health services have been improving as a result of various pragmatic measures adopted by the government. For instance, to meet the shortage of facilities in rural and tribal areas, a health corps was organized in 1964, and its 400 units had established clinics and health centres that provided outpatient treatment to more than half of the villages by the early 1970s. Various organizations offered health and welfare services and operated orphanages and sanatoriums. Over the years, there have been increases in government investment in the health sector; in the financial year 1993/94, for example, a little over 7 per cent of the total budgeted expenditure of the central government was allocated to health services.

The Master Plan of Health, 1983-2002, reflects the constitutional provision for health in the form of practical strategies by focusing on the needs of deprived and underserved persons; special attention is given to the needs of mothers and children in the allocation of resources. According to data from the Statistical Centre, in 1992 the country had 680 government hospitals and nursing homes providing residential care, in addition to 118 private facilities and 67 charity-run institutions. A further 12,220 health houses and 4,000 health centres operated in rural and urban areas. The 1992 cadre of health personnel included 18,000 registered doctors, or one doctor per 3,120 people, and an estimated 105,000 paramedics. Currently, over 75 per cent of the rural and 60 per cent of the urban population are served by the established health network of the Ministry of Health and Medical Education. The employment of trained female volunteers in suburban areas, large cities and deprived rural areas is an important step towards enhancing the accessibility of health care in the country.

The Ministry of Health and Medical Education is responsible for funding and managing the national health care system. Private institutions generally charge for their services and there is a system of subscriptions paid by employers for private insurance schemes. Charitable institutions benefit from a combination of fees and donations and, in the case of Islamic institutions, are also eligible to receive funds raised through the Shia tax of *Khums*.

In 1986, about 74 per cent of regular settled households had access to piped water supply, this proportion being higher in urban areas (89.3 per cent) than in rural areas (51.5 per cent). For the country as a whole, about 95 per cent of the regular dwelling units were supplied with sanitary toilets, the proportion being 97.7 per cent in the urban areas and 91.2 per cent in the rural areas.

C. WOMEN'S PROFILE

1. Demographic characteristics

(a) Gender balance

According to the data from censuses and surveys, males have consistently outnumbered females in the total population. In 1991, there were 106.3 males per 100 females, or 94.1 females for every 100 males in the country. There have, however, been fluctuations in these ratios over the years; the sex ratio, or number of males per 100 females, of 106.3 in 1991 was significantly higher than the ratio of 103.6 in 1956 (table 5). The higher than expected sex ratio in the Iranian population may be attributed to two important factors: higher female than male mortality; and possible greater under-enumeration of females at the censuses.

Males also outnumber females in both urban and rural areas, but the excess of males is more pronounced in urban than in rural areas. For instance, the 1976 census reported a sex ratio of 109.6 males per 100 females in urban areas, which was considerably higher than the ratio of 103.1 reported for rural areas. The very high sex ratio in urban areas could be explained in terms of a preponderance of males

Table 5. Numerical and percentage distribution of the enumerated population and gender-balance ratios: 1956-1991

Census year	Enumerated population						Gender ratio	
	Both sexes		Male		Female		Males per 100 females	Females per 100 males
	Number	Percent-age	Number	Percent-age	Number	Percent-age		
1956	18 954 704	100.0	9 644 944	50.9	9 309 760	49.1	103.6	96.5
1966	25 788 722	100.0	13 355 801	51.8	12 432 921	48.2	107.4	93.1
1976	33 708 744	100.0	17 356 347	51.5	16 352 397	48.5	106.1	94.2
1986	49 445 010	100.0	25 280 961	51.1	24 164 049	48.9	104.6	95.6
1991	55 837 163	100.0	28 768 450	51.5	27 068 713	48.5	106.3	94.1

Source: Statistical Centre of Iran, *A Statistical Reflection of the Islamic Republic of Iran,* No. 12, December 1995.

among the rural-to-urban migrants. However, since 1976, the urban-rural differential in the sex ratio has been narrowing and, according to the 1991 multi-round survey, the urban ratio of 106.7 was only slightly higher than the rural ratio of 105.7, suggesting an increase in the proportionate share of females in the rural-to-urban migrant streams over the years (table 6).

The extent of male excess in the total population also varies across the 24 provinces. In 1986, for instance, the sex ratio ranged from a low of around 101.5 in Sistan and Baluchestan and Mazandaran provinces to a high of 107 or more in Esafahan, Hamadan, Ilam, Kohgiluyeh and Boyer Ahmad provinces (annex tables C.1 and C.2).

The sex ratio also varies among the various age groups, but does not show any uniform pat-

tern over the years. For instance, there was an excess of females over males at ages 20-34 years at the 1976 census, and at ages 34-39 years and 75 years and over at the 1986 census, but according to the 1991 census data males outnumber females in all age groups (table 7).

(b) Age structure

The numerical and percentage distribution of the total as well as male and female population by conventional five-year age groups is given in annex tables C.3 and C.4. Like other developing countries with high fertility, the population of the Islamic Republic of Iran is still very young in that children and youth below 20 years of age constituted 54.9 per cent of the total population in 1991, this proportion being slightly lower for males (54.6 per cent) than for females (54.9 per cent). It is also evident from annex

Table 6. Numerical and percentage distribution of the population by sex and residence and gender ratio: 1956-1991

Census year	Urban areas					Rural areas				
	Population (thousands)		Gender ratio			Population (thousands)		Gender ratio		
	Male	Female	Percent-age female	Males per 100 females	Females per 100 males	Male	Female	Percent-age female	Males per 100 females	Females per 100 males
1956	3 070	2 883	48.4	106.5	93.9	6 575	6 426	49.4	102.3	97.7
1966	5 097	4 697	48.0	108.5	92.2	8 259	7 735	48.4	106.8	93.7
1976	8 291	7 563	47.7	109.6	91.2	9 065	8 789	49.2	103.1	97.0
1986	13 770	13 075	48.7	105.3	95.0	11 387	10 965	49.1	103.8	96.3
1991	16 435	15 401	48.4	106.7	93.7	12 145	11 492	48.6	105.7	94.6

Source: Statistical Centre of Iran, *A Statistical Reflection of the Islamic Republic of Iran,* No. 12, December 1995.

Table 7. Sex ratio (males per 100 females) by age group: 1976, 1986 and 1991

Age group	1976	1986	1991
0-4	108.2	103.3	104.3
5-9	107.1	104.4	104.3
10-14	110.8	107.2	107.0
15-19	101.9	105.1	107.2
20-24	93.3	100.7	103.8
25-29	92.0	100.5	101.0
30-34	96.6	81.7	103.2
35-39	102.8	97.3	104.1
40-44	115.8	101.5	101.7
45-49	118.4	106.9	102.4
50-54	122.0	115.5	109.7
55-59	128.9	115.0	122.1
60-64	108.9	122.3	124.7
65-69	109.4	117.0	138.5
70-74	103.5	104.8	131.7
75-79	129.6	94.4	125.3
80-84	117.2	87.8	110.4
85+	115.1	99.0	106.0
All ages	106.2	104.6	106.3

Source: Statistical Centre of Iran.

Table 8. Percentage distribution of the population by broad age group and by sex, and dependency ratio: 1986 and 1991

Age group	1986 Both sexes	1986 Male	1986 Female	1991 Both sexes	1991 Male	1991 Female
0-14	45.4	45.5	45.5	44.3	44.0	44.4
15-59	49.1	48.8	49.2	49.9	49.7	50.1
60+	5.5	5.7	5.3	5.8	6.3	5.5
All ages	100.0	100.0	100.0	100.0	100.0	100.0
Dependency ratio	103.8	104.6	103.0	100.4	101.0	99.3

Source: Statistical Centre of Iran.

tables C.3 and C.4 that between 1986 and 1991 there was a slight decline in the number as well as relative share of children aged 0-4 years, reflecting the decline in fertility in recent years, and an increase in the number and proportionate share of children aged 5-14 years. During the same six-year period, women in reproductive ages 15-49 years as a proportion of all women had also increased, from 43.9 to 45.1 per cent.

The percentage distribution of the population according to three broad age groups, 0-14 (child population), 15-59 (working age population) and 60 and over (elderly population), is given in table 8.

It will be noted from table 8 that between 1986 and 1991, while the proportionate share of children had decreased, that of the working-age population had increased slightly among both males and females. The increase in the proportions of persons in the working-age groups has resulted in a decline in the dependency ratio, or the ratio of persons in the "dependent" ages (0-14 and 60+) to those in the economically productive or working ages (15-59 years). Since the proportionate share of the working-age population is slightly higher among females

than among males, the total dependency ratio for females was lower than that for males in 1986 as well as in 1991.

There are significant differences in the proportionate shares of the three broad age groups between urban and rural areas. For example, in 1991, the proportion of children aged 0-14 years in rural areas (46-9 per cent) was 4.8 percentage points higher than the corresponding proportion in urban areas (42.1 per cent), and this differential was more marked among males (5.2 percentage points) than females (4.2 percentage points). The higher proportion of children in rural compared with urban areas reflects the higher rural than urban fertility. The proportion of the elderly in rural areas (6.2 per cent) was only slightly higher than in urban areas (5.5 per cent). Consequently, persons in working ages (15-59 years) constituted 52.4 per cent or 5.5 percentage points higher in urban areas compared with 46.9 per cent in rural areas, due also partly to the fact that persons in the young working-age groups constitute the majority of the rural-to-urban migrants. Since the proportion of the working-age population is higher in urban than in rural areas, dependency ratios are lower in urban compared with rural areas (table 9).

(c) Marital status

The numerical and percentage distribution of the population aged 10 years and over by marital status and gender is given in table 10.

Table 9. Percentage distribution of the population by broad age group and by sex, and dependency ratios in urban and rural areas: 1991

Age group	Urban areas			Rural areas		
	Both sexes	Male	Female	Both sexes	Male	Female
0-14	42.1	41.6	42.7	46.9	46.8	46.9
15-59	52.4	52.6	52.3	46.9	46.3	47.5
60+	5.5	5.8	5.0	6.2	6.9	5.6
Total	100.0	100.0	100.0	100.0	100.0	100.0
Dependency ratio	90.7	90.1	91.2	113.7	115.8	110.7

Source: Statistical Centre of Iran.

It will be noted that nearly 56 per cent of females aged 10 years and over as against 52 per cent of males were reported to be married in 1991, and those proportions were significantly lower than the corresponding proportions in 1986. Simultaneously, there has been an increase in the proportions never married, from 41.6 to 45.5 per cent for males and from 32.0 to 36.6 per cent for females.

It is also clear from table 10 that the incidence of widowhood is considerably higher among females than among males, although the proportion widowed among females had declined from 7.0 per cent in 1986 to 5.9 per cent in 1991. The significantly higher incidence of widowhood among females is due to several factors. In the first instance, mortality among males is now considered to be higher than among females, and this, together with the fact that Iranian women generally marry men several years their senior in age, results in a higher incidence of widowhood among women. Second, in cases where a man has more than one wife, his death will result in two or more women being widowed. Another important reason is that, as in many other countries of the region, widowed men have better chances of remarrying and thus ending their widowhood than widowed females.

2. Educational background

Historically, women had been deprived of education in the Islamic Republic of Iran. Socio-cultural values and customs had prevented girls from entering and finishing school. In recent years, however, the government has issued policy guidelines on the importance of educating women. The policy emphasizes that the education system should duly recognize the identity of women and their role in family and society on the basis of Islam, and plan for the method and content of their schooling accordingly. The policy also stresses that the system of education should take into consideration the unique characteristics of boys and girls by preparing them for their different roles in the family and society.

The strong commitment of the government to improve women's access to and participation

Table 10. Numerical and percentage distribution of the population aged 10 years and over by marital status and sex: 1986 and 1991

Marital status	1986				1991			
	Male		Female		Male		Female	
	Number (thousands)	Percentage	Number (thousands)	Percentage	Number (thousands)	Percentage	Number (thousands)	Percentage
Married	9 179	54.5	9 367	58.4	10 443	52.2	10 433	55.9
Widowed	218	1.3	1 123	7.0	272	1.4	1 107	5.9
Divorced	62	0.4	103	0.6	50	0.3	82	0.4
Never married	7 012	41.6	5 128	32.0	9 106	45.5	6 833	36.6
Not reported	369	2.2	310	1.9	126	0.6	202	1.1
All statuses	16 840	100.0	16 031	100.0	19 997	100.0	18 657	100.0

Source: Statistical Centre of Iran, *A Statistical Reflection of the Islamic Republic of Iran*, Nos. 9 and 12.

in education as well as public investments in appropriate facilities had resulted in noteworthy progress being made in regard to female education during the past two decades. In addition, the increasing support of parents for their daughters' education and notable enthusiasm on the part of the girls themselves to pursue their education had resulted in the rising participation of girls in the education system and in a gradual narrowing of the gender gap in regard to educational enrolment and attainment over the past two decades or more. Available information also indicates that the academic performance of female students is, on the average, five percentage points higher than that of their male counterparts.

(a) Educational participation

According to data from the Ministry of Education, total enrolments at the primary level of education increased dramatically from about 4.8 million in 1976/77 to about 9.9 million in 1993/94, reflecting a doubling of enrolments in 17 years. But this increase was more marked in the case of females than males; while the enrolment of boys increased from about 2.9 million to 5.2 million, or by 77.2 per cent, female enrolments more than doubled (or increased by 154.4 per cent) from about 1.8 million to about 4.7 million during the same period. Consequently, the relative share of females in total primary-level enrolment increased from 38.4 per cent in 1976/77 to 47.2 per cent in 1993/94 (table 11).

Student enrolments at the secondary level also increased rapidly between 1976/77 and 1993/94, and this increase was more pronounced in the case of girls than boys. At the junior secondary level, while enrolment of males increased by 185 per cent, that of females increased by 202 per cent; and consequently, the relative share of females in total junior secondary enrolments rose from 36.0 per cent in 1976/77 to 43.3 per cent in 1993/94. At the senior secondary level also, since female enrolments increased faster (by about 202 per cent) than male enrolments (138 per cent), the proportionate share of females in total senior secondary level enrolments increased from 39.6 to 45.4 per cent during the same 17-year period (table 12).

In recent years, there has also been a dramatic increase in female enrolment in university or higher levels of education, with their numbers more than doubling from 84,912 in 1988/89 to 177,328 in 1993/94. Despite such increases, women remain very much under-represented in higher education, constituting only about 31 per cent of total enrolments at this level in 1993/94. This proportion was considerably higher in the private universities (37.9 per cent) compared with the public universities (28.4 per cent) in the same year (table 13).

Although there have been considerable improvements in the enrolment of girls in primary education, their participation decreases with increases in the level of education; this is particularly true in rural areas. The decrease in the proportionate share of females in total enrolments at higher levels of education has been the result of several factors. First, the higher education of girls brings no direct benefit to the parental family because soon after puberty

Table 11. Student enrolments at primary education level by sex: selected years, 1976/77 to 1993/94

Year	Both sexes		Male		Female	
	Number	Percent-age	Number	Percent-age	Number	Percent-age
1976/77	4 768 588	100.0	2 939 800	61.6	1 828 788	38.4
1986/87	7 232 820	100.0	4 058 853	56.1	3 173 967	43.9
1991/92	9 787 593	100.0	5 224 343	53.4	4 563 250	46.6
1993/94	9 862 617	100.0	5 210 412	52.8	4 652 205	47.2

Source: Ministry of Education.

**Table 12. Student enrolments at junior secondary and senior secondary levels by sex:
selected years, 1976/77 to 1993/94**

Year	Junior secondary				Senior secondary			
	Both sexes	Male	Female	Percent-age female	Both sexes	Male	Female	Percent-age female
1976/77	1 368 910	875 156	493 394	36.0	740 471	446 974	293 497	39.6
1986/87	2 299 510	1 406 118	893 392	38.9	1 076 762	614 026	462 736	43.0
1991/92	3 541 578	2 050 707	1 490 871	42.1	1 770 410	984 218	786 192	44.4
1993/94	4 420 971	2 496 712	1 924 259	43.5	1 948 203	1 062 714	885 489	45.4

Source: Ministry of Education.

Table 13. Student enrolments in public and private universities by sex: 1988/89 to 1993/94

Year	Public universities			Private universities			All universities		
	Both sexes	Female	Percent-age female	Both sexes	Female	Percent-age female	Both sexes	Female	Percent-age female
1988/89	250 709	71 822	28.6	39 270	13 090	33.3	289 979	84 912	29.3
1989/90	281 385	78 568	27.9	66 268	24 107	36.4	347 653	102 675	29.5
1990/91	312 076	85 325	27.3	87 021	32 370	37.2	399 097	117 695	29.5
1991/92	344 045	96 969	28.2	77 907	31 937	41.0	421 952	128 906	30.5
1992/93	374 734	105 667	28.2	115 294	46 263	40.1	490 028	151 930	31.0
1993/94	436 564	125 350	28.7	139 761	52 978	37.9	576 325	178 328	30.9

Sources: Ministry of Culture and Higher Education; and Islamic Azad University.

a daughter is expected to be married and leave the parental home. On the other hand, by remaining at home the young girl not only helps her mother in domestic chores but is also able to learn home management, which is considered a positive qualification for marriage. Second, the national education policy as well as the school curricula promote the domestic role of women as against their participation in employment outside the home. Third, parents are reluctant to send their daughters to secondary and higher educational institutions if these facilities are located far away from their homes. Fourth, most girls in rural areas marry in their teens, and young married girls are usually deprived of school education since, as noted earlier, they are not permitted to attend schools along with unmarried girls; and co-education is also not permitted.

An interesting feature of enrolments in higher educational institutions in the Islamic Republic of Iran, as in most other countries of the region, is the general tendency for students to pursue fields of study conforming to socially defined feminine and masculine roles. For instance, according to the 1993/94 data on student enrolments at the universities, 52.3 per cent of female students as against 43.5 per cent of male students were enrolled in humanities/social sciences and arts courses. The data also show that while the proportion enrolled in basic sciences is significantly higher among females (15.9 per cent) than among males (11.1 per cent), there is gross under-representation of females in agriculture and veterinary sciences as well as technical and engineering courses; females constitute about 5-6 per cent of the total enrolments in these courses of study. It is also interesting to note that females account for 48.2 per cent of total enrolments in medical sciences (table 14). The relatively very high proportion of females among medical science students is largely due to the fact that since

Table 14. Distribution of student enrolments in universities by sex and course of study: 1993/94

Course of study	Both sexes		Male		Female	
	Number	Percent-age	Number	Percent-age	Number	Percent-age
Humanities/social sciences	257 608	44.7	168 295	42.2	89 313	50.4
Basic sciences	72 668	12.6	44 403	11.1	28 265	15.9
Agriculture and veterinary	29 684	5.2	28 105	7.0	1 579	0.9
Technical and engineering	108 331	18.8	101 343	25.4	6 988	3.9
Medical sciences	99 468	17.3	51 571	12.9	47 897	27.0
Arts	8 566	1.5	5 280	1.3	3 286	1.9
Total	576 325	100.0	398 997	100.0	177 328	100.0

Sources: Ministry of Culture and Higher Education; and Islamic Azad University.

1993 an equal number of males and females are being admitted to these courses.

Available information also suggests that women are either debarred or discouraged from studying and obtaining training in the specialized fields of engineering, agriculture and veterinary medicine. Of the 431 fields of study in the universities, 123 fields have no female enrolment. This limits the opportunity for women to develop the usable skills needed for employment.

(b) Educational attainment

An important indicator of the educational attainment of a population is the literacy rate, or the percentage of the population above a defined minimum age that is literate. The total as well as literate population aged six years and over by gender and residence are given in annex table C.5. The literacy rates by sex and residence for 1976, 1981 and 1991 are shown in table 15.

It will be noted from table 15 that the literacy rates of persons aged six years and over increased rapidly between 1976 and 1991, and that this increase was more pronounced for females than for males. For males, the literacy rate increased from 58.9 per cent in 1976 to 80.6 per cent in 1991, while for females it rose from 35.4 to 67.4 per cent over the same period. Consequently, the gender gap in literacy rates decreased from 23.5 percentage points in 1976 to 13.2 percentage points in 1991.

It is also evident from table 15 that although there have been increases in the literacy rates in both urban and rural areas, these increases have been faster in rural than in urban areas for males as well as females. The increase was particularly significant in respect of rural females, whose literacy rate more than trebled from 17.3 per cent in 1976 to 54.2 per cent in 1991. Nevertheless, literacy rates have always been considerably higher in urban than

Table 15. Literacy rates of persons aged six years and over by sex and residence: 1971, 1986 and 1991

Year	Iran			Urban areas			Rural areas		
	Both sexes	Male	Female	Both sexes	Male	Female	Both sexes	Male	Female
1976	47.4	58.9	35.4	65.4	74.4	55.6	30.5	43.6	17.3
1986	61.8	71.0	52.1	73.1	80.3	65.4	48.4	64.6	36.3
1991	74.1	80.6	67.4	81.9	86.7	76.8	63.7	72.6	54.2

Source: Statistical Centre of Iran.

in rural areas. In 1991, the urban female literacy rate was 22.6 percentage points higher than the rural female rate.

3. Health status

(a) Maternal health

A systematic analysis of trends in levels and causes of maternal mortality in the Islamic Republic of Iran is to a large extent handicapped by the lack of reliable and up-to-date data and information. Nevertheless, attempts have been made to estimate maternal mortality rates on the basis of relevant data obtained from hospital records and through sample investigations. For instance, a limited analysis based on records maintained by Saadi Hospital, Pahlavi University revealed a maternal mortality rate per 100,000 live births of 392 during the period 1963-1969 and of 249 during the period 1970-1976. A more comprehensive analysis based on data from a 10 per cent sample survey covering all urban and all rural areas (except Kurdistan) between 1984 and 1985 reported a maternal mortality rate per 100,000 live births of 233 in rural areas and 77 in urban areas. According to a second round of this survey carried out between 1986 and 1987, the maternal mortality rate was found to be 184 in rural areas and 63 in urban areas (table 16).

Table 16. Maternal mortality rate (per 100,000 live births) by residence: 1984/85 and 1986/87

Residence	1984/85	1986/87
Iran	136	120
Urban	77	63
Rural	233	184

Sources: H. Malek-Afzali, "Birth and death indicators in the Islamic Republic of Iran in 1984 and 1986", *Medical Journal of the Islamic Republic of Iran*, vol. 2, No. 4 (1988).

The limited information available indicates that about two decades ago the maternal mortality rate in the Islamic Republic of Iran was very high, particularly in the rural areas, and this high rate has been attributed to lack of coverage of medical care services. For instance,

estimates indicate that only a very small proportion of birth deliveries, especially in rural areas, took place under the supervision of trained health personnel. However, since 1985, with the expansion of primary health care services in rural areas and the increased frequency of the presence of trained personnel during delivery, there has been a very significant decrease in the maternal mortality rate, which in 1991 was estimated to be 26 per 100,000 live births in urban and 57 in rural areas (table 17). The implementation of the family planning programme has also contributed to a reduction in maternal mortality through lowering the number of births occurring to a woman during her reproductive years. Besides the improvement in primary health care facilities, other factors, such as rapid urbanization, improvement in road communications, which facilitates hospital deliveries, have also contributed positively to the reduction in maternal mortality over the years.

Table 17. Estimated maternal mortality rates for urban and rural areas: selected years, 1974-1991

(Per 100,000 live births)

Year	Urban	Rural
1974	120	370
1985	77	233
1988	41	138
1991	26	57

Source: United Nations Children's Fund, *Situation Analysis of Women and Children in Iran, 1992.*

Although there have been significant improvements in the maternal mortality rate, there are still marked disparities in these rates between urban and rural areas. Estimates indicate that in 1991, the rural maternal mortality rate of 57 per 100,000 live births was more than double the rate of 26 for urban areas (table 17). There are also significant regional variations ranging from 11 to more than 100 per 100,000 live births in some provinces, where a significant proportion of deliveries occur under the care of untrained birth attendants. At the national level, the proportion of deliveries attended by such attendants was 17.5 per cent, but varied from 4.0 to 56.5 per cent.

The Islamic Republic of Iran has yet to undertake a comprehensive national survey to ascertain the prevalence of maternal morbidity and its causes, common diseases, gynaecological problems among women, as well as the nutritional levels of mothers during and after childbirth. However, information obtained through small-scale and localized studies indicates a high prevalence of iron deficiency anaemia among 20-30 per cent of pregnant women owing largely to poor dietary habits, parasitic infections and multiple parity. Available evidence also suggests that the leading cause of maternal mortality, particularly in rural areas, is haemorrhage during and after delivery.

(b) Infant and child health

Available data and information point to an impressive improvement in the health condition of infants and children during the past two decades. These improvements are reflected in the sharp declines in infant and child mortality rates as well as in the enhanced nutritional status of these population groups.

The infant mortality rate (IMR), estimated at 120 per thousand live births in 1956, had declined to 37.3 in 1992, and with the exception of a few underserved provinces, IMR is today below the goal of 50 set by the World Summit for Children. Available estimates also indicate that in the past, mortality was significantly higher among female compared with male infants; in 1978, the mortality rate was 96 per thousand live births among female infants and 86 among male infants. However, this gender differential has been narrowing over the years,

and in 1993 the estimated female IMR of 33 per thousand live births was slightly lower than the male rate of 34 per thousand (table 18).

According to available estimates, the child mortality rate is now lower than it was before the expansion of health care services. The mortality rates of children have been more than halved in 15 years, from 90 per thousand in 1978 to 41 per thousand in 1993 (table 18).

Table 18. Estimated infant and child mortality rates: selected years, 1978 to 1993

Year	Infant mortality rate		Child mortality rate
	Male	Female	
1978	86	96	90
1984	46	45	56
1993	34	33	41

Source: Ministry of Health and Medical Education.

Several factors have contributed to the remarkable decline in infant and child mortality. First, there has been considerable expansion in immunization against the diseases which are controlled by vaccines in urban as well as rural areas. In 1993, an estimated 85 per cent of children were immunized against vaccine-controlled diseases through routine vaccination. In 1992, the percentage of children under one year of age fully immunized against these diseases was about the same in rural as in urban areas (table 19). Meanwhile, the successful campaign against polio, which was

Table 19. Percentage of children under one year old fully immunized against vaccine-preventable diseases by residence: 1987 and 1992

Vaccine-preventable disease	1987			1992		
	Iran	Urban	Rural	Iran	Urban	Rural
Tuberculosis (TB)	65	53	77	92	91	93
Polio	67	63	70	87	87	88
DPT	67	63	70	87	87	88
Measles	63	54	71	84	83	85

Source: Ministry of Health and Medical Education.

launched in April 1994, succeeded in eradicating this disease by 1996. The percentage of pregnant women fully immunized against tetanus increased from 40 in 1987 to 78 in 1992.

Relevant indicators also point towards considerable improvement in the nutritional status of infants and children in the country. For instance, the proportion of children who are breastfed for a period of at least 12 months increased from 65 per cent in 1987 to 67 per cent in 1993, while the proportion receiving supplemental food appropriate for their age had increased from 29 to 56 per cent during the same six-year period. A specific indicator of the improved nutrition of pregnant women is the fact that currently 92 per cent of infants weigh over 2,500 grams at birth.

Despite the improvements in nutritional status, comprehensive health survey data indicate that problems of malnutrition exist among children in both urban and rural areas. For instance, malnutrition among children under five years of age was reported to be 7 per cent in urban areas and 12 per cent in rural areas of Tehran Province, the comparable figures for Sistan-Baluchestan Province being 35 and 42 per cent respectively. The survey also shows a clear disparity in the nutritional status of boys and girls. In the rural areas, for instance, 20 per cent of girls were found to be malnourished as against 13 per cent of boys. Several studies have also reported a tendency towards discrimination in breastfeeding in favour of boys in rural areas.

(c) Life expectancy

According to estimates prepared by the United Nations, female life expectancy was either equal to or lower than male life expectancy until about the early 1970s. Since then, with increasing health care and attention given to mothers and women, female life expectancy has been increasing slightly faster than male life expectancy, and in the period 1990-1995 the estimated female life expectancy at birth of 68.0 years was slightly longer than the 67.0 years for males (table 20).

D. WOMEN IN FAMILY LIFE

1. The Iranian family

In the Islamic Republic of Iran, as in practically all other countries, the family continues to be the basic unit of society, serving as the shelter for its members and providing them with identity, security and social orientation. By and large, the organizational principles of the Iranian family have traditionally been patrilineal descent and patrilineal residence. These principles mean that membership in the kinship group is determined by descent through males and not females; formal authority is vested in the males; males are primary property holders and property inheritors; and sons and their wives and children would usually live in their father's household or in the same compound. These basic determinants of family organization have, however, varied somewhat among religious and ethnic groups.

Table 20. Estimated life expectancy at birth by sex: 1950-1955 to 1990-1995

Sex	Life expectancy at birth (years)								
	1950-1955	1955-1960	1960-1965	1965-1970	1970-1975	1975-1980	1980-1985	1985-1990	1990-1995
Both sexes	46.1	48.3	50.8	53.2	55.9	58.6	61.2	65.2	67.5
Males	46.1	48.3	50.9	53.5	56.2	58.2	59.4	65.0	67.0
Females	46.1	48.3	50.6	52.9	55.5	59.0	63.0	65.5	68.0

Source: United Nations.

Traditionally, the extended family, comprising a couple, their unmarried children, and married sons with their spouses and children, had been the most common family type among almost all segments of the Iranian people. This family structure, which had gained early acceptance in a predominantly agrarian society, was later reinforced by Islamic tenets and practices. The traditional extended family performed numerous economic, religious, political, social and educational functions. The head of the family was almost always the oldest male member, who commanded obedience and respect from other family members and who was responsible for the management of the internal and external affairs of the family. Among family members, status and authority were always determined by both age and sex, with the older dominating the younger, and the males dominating the females. While all able-bodied male members worked together to support the family in its economic activities, women were generally expected to fulfil their obligations as mothers and wives.

The 1928 Civil Code of Iran and subsequent amendments to the Code assert that the family is based upon the harmonious coexistence of husband and wife. The Code permits men and women the same rights of property ownership and voting rights, but differential legal rights exist in favour of men in marriage and divorce law, custody and guardianship of children, inheritance, nationality, and marriage alimony. The Religious Law, which has not been contradicted by civil law, defines a wife's relation to her husband as one of submission, apparently implying that the husband has the right to expect his wife to perform her wifely duties, which involve responsibility for domestic chores and care of children, as well as her willingness to provide sexual gratification. By her action and behaviour both at home and in public, a women must help her husband to maintain his status and, in effect, the status of the family.

Although traditionally the civil rights of women have been minimal, Iranian women as individuals are often not as completely passive and subordinate as is sometimes believed. Studies have reported that a woman can have an important say in deliberations and decisions concerning domestic matters, and that mothers exercise a profound and persistent influence on their sons. More often than not, it is the woman who influences the choice of brides for her sons and grooms for her daughters. The extent to which a woman can influence decision-making depends on the nature of the relationship she has built through years of association with her husband, brothers and adult sons. In other words, the image of the Iranian family system as a rigidly and unexceptionally male-dominated system is exaggerated.

Over the years, however, there have been several fundamental changes in the structure and functions of the traditional family as a result of social reforms instituted from time to time, as well as the influence of Western thought and norms, industrialization and urbanization. The nuclear or conjugal family, comprising parents and their unmarried children, has become increasingly more common, particularly in urban areas. There have also been changes in attitudes and hierarchical relationships within the family, and in certain situations women have become heads of households. For instance, according to the 1991 multi-round population survey, 630,038, or 5.9 per cent, of the 10,758,321 households in the country were headed by women.

The 1991 survey data also revealed that among the female household heads, the majority (67.5 per cent) were aged 50 years and over and 40 per cent were living alone or in one-member households (table 21). The survey also showed that about 80 per cent of the female household heads were widows, suggesting that women normally assume headship of the household only upon the death of their husbands.

In 1991, about 26 per cent of all female household heads were reported to be literate, the proportion being 36.3 per cent in urban areas and 9.0 per cent in rural areas. Only 11.6 per cent of the female heads of households were employed, and the remaining 88.4 per cent were not engaged in any economic activity outside their homes.

Table 21. Numerical and percentage distribution of female-headed households by age group

Age of household head (years)	Household size (number of persons per household)								Percentage of total
	1	2	3	4	5	6	7 and over	Total	
<20	2 679	1 960	1 270	697	319	197	213	7 335	1.1
20-29	4 291	6 532	7 705	5 768	3 505	2 005	1 289	31 095	4.9
30-39	5 470	8 272	12 913	14 645	13 122	10 223	11 174	75 819	11.9
40-49	9 992	13 087	16 653	16 419	13 435	10 279	12 423	92 288	14.5
50-59	39 221	32 168	27 387	19 186	12 023	6 664	6 310	142 959	22.4
60 and over	191 313	51 356	22 457	10 908	5 609	3 139	2 893	287 675	45.1
Unspecified	588	81	53	40	42	25	38	867	0.1
Total	253 554	113 456	88 438	67 663	48 055	32 532	34 340	638 038	100.0
Percentage of total	39.7	17.8	13.9	10.6	7.5	5.1	5.4	100.0	–

Source: Statistical Centre of Iran.

2. Family formation

(a) Marriage patterns

In the Islamic Republic of Iran, as in most other countries of the region, marriage has been universal. Parents have always considered it their prime responsibility to have their sons and daughters married soon after they reached marriageable age. Consequently, the marriage rate, or the proportion of persons above a minimum age who were married, was relatively high. For instance, according to the 1996 census, 56.5 per cent of males and 61.0 per cent of females aged 10 years and over were reported to be married. The census also revealed that nearly 72 per cent of the males and 94 per cent of the females were married at ages 25-29 years, and that the highest marriage rates were 94.7 per cent at ages 30-34 years for females, and 95.7 per cent at ages 30-49 years for males. The proportion married was also significantly higher in rural than in urban areas: about 52 per cent of males and 57 per cent of females aged 10 years and over were married in urban areas, compared with 60 and 64 per cent respectively in rural areas. Estimates also indicate that only less than 1 person in 10 remained unmarried or single.

Although the legal minimum age at marriage was 16 for girls and 18 for boys, early marriages, especially of girls, were common, particularly in rural areas. The traditional practice has been for a girl to be betrothed at birth

and married as soon as she attained puberty, at ages 13 or 14 years. Early betrothals were also more likely between kinsmen, particularly cousins, than with outsiders. However, among some ethnic groups, as for example the nomadic Bessari who live near Shiraz, girls were generally more than 16 years old when they were given in marriage. Generally, men marry well after the minimum legal age of 18 years. According to the 1966 census, about 45 per cent of girls aged 15-19 years were married, the corresponding proportion among boys being 4.2 per cent.

By and large, parents have been arranging the marriages of their children, the selection of a marriage partner being determined by customary preference, economic circumstances and geographic considerations. Despite the fact that the consent of the prospective groom and bride was a legal prerequisite of marriage, the choice of a spouse for the son or daughter had almost always been a matter of parental discretion. The law also requires a girl to obtain parental permission in order to marry, but this requirement is not applicable to boys.

Marriages between relatives, especially between paternal cousins, had for long been common among a substantial section of the Iranians, because consanguineous marriages not only helped to strengthen intra-family solidarity but also usually entailed less of an economic burden on the husband and his parents. According to a study based on the 1976/77 Iran Fertility Survey data, almost 40 per cent of ever-married women aged 15-50 years reported having married a relative, 24 per cent to a close relative and 16 per cent to a distant relative. The study also found that despite modernization and enhanced social status, there was a modest increase in the proportion of marriages of cousins between the 1940s and the 1970s, possibly because of the increased availability of first cousins of marriageable age (Givens and Hirschman: 1994).

In recent years, however, significant changes have taken place in regard to marriage patterns and practices in the country. For instance, the incidence of consanguineous marriages has decreased considerably, and today the practice is very much less frequent in towns and cities compared with rural areas. Second, there is now more freedom in selecting marriage partners, with boys and girls having a greater say in the final decision. Third, the growing number of Iranian youth going abroad for studies has resulted in an increase in the number of mixed marriages between Iranians and other nationals, especially Europeans and Americans.

Another important development in the Islamic Republic of Iran, as in several other Asian countries, is the growing tendency among young men and women to delay their marriage because of schooling, employment or military service. This tendency is reflected in an increase in the mean age at first marriage, especially of females, which increased steadily from 18.4 years in 1976 to 20.9 in 1991, and further to 21.6 years in 1993 (table 22). This increase has also been partly due to the fact that amendments to the family code ratified in

1975 and 1976 raised the minimum age at marriage to 18 years for females.

The increasing tendency to delay marriage is also reflected in the proportion of the population reported as married or ever-married at successive censuses or surveys. Between 1986 and 1991, the proportion of persons aged 10 years and over who were married declined from 56.5 to 52.2 per cent for males and from 61.0 to 55.9 per cent for females. These declines have been more pronounced in respect of persons at prime marriage ages 15-19 and 20-24 years. For instance, between 1986 and 1991 the proportion of ever-married among women decreased from 35.5 to 25.5 per cent at ages 15-19 years, and from 73.6 to 67.1 per cent at ages 20-24 years. A similar decrease has been reported in respect of currently married women between 1986 and 1991 in both urban and rural areas (table 23).

(b) Reproductive behaviour

In addition to shifts in marriage patterns, there have been significant changes in the reproductive behaviour of Iranian women in recent decades. In particular, the attitude of married couples towards desired family size has undergone significant transformation, as is evidenced by the decline in the number of children parents produce and the increasing acceptance of family planning by Iranian women.

In the absence of reliable registration data on birth and deaths, attempts have been made to estimate the total fertility rate (TFR), or the

Table 22. Mean age at first marriage by sex and residence: 1966-1993

Year	Iran		Urban		Rural	
	Male	Female	Male	Female	Male	Female
1966	–	18.4	–	–	–	–
1976	24.0	19.7	25.1	20.2	22.7	19.1
1986	23.8	19.9	24.4	28.2	22.8	19.6
1991	24.4	21.1	21.1	23.2	20.8	–
1993	–	21.6	–	–	–	–

Source: Statistical Centre of Iran.

Table 23. Percentage of currently married among females aged 15-49 years by five-year age group and residence: 1986 and 1991

Age group	Iran		Urban		Rural	
	1986	1991	1986	1991	1986	1991
15-19	33.2	25.1	31.8	24.2	34.0	25.9
20-24	72.6	66.3	73.9	66.1	73.8	66.5
25-29	90.0	86.1	87.1	85.6	89.8	87.0
30-34	92.1	92.0	91.5	91.4	93.5	93.3
35-39	92.2	93.1	92.2	92.5	94.0	94.2
40-44	90.1	91.6	91.2	91.0	92.4	92.7
45-49	83.7	89.0	88.5	87.0	89.3	90.5
15-49	72.4	70.2	72.9	71.2	73.3	68.8

Source: Akbar Aghajanian, "A new direction in population policy and family planning in the Islamic Republic of Iran", *Asia-Pacific Population Journal,* vol. 10, No. 1 (1995).

number of children ever-born per ever-married woman, on the basis of relevant data and information obtained through censuses and surveys. However, because of the differences in methods of calculation, there are slight differences in the estimates of TFR derived by various sources (table 24).

It will be noted from table 24 that, despite differences in values, all three independent estimates point to a very significant decline in TFR since the mid-1960s, but that this decline has not been continuous. TFR declined substantially between 1966 and 1976, but rose again between 1976 and 1986, thereafter declining gradually. These fluctuations have largely been due to conflicting policies and views espoused by the different regimes.

During the period 1966-1976, socio-economic changes, such as the high rate of economic growth, industrialization, urbanization and increase in female education and employment, were favourable to the onset of fertility decline. The family planning programme implemented during this period also helped to increase the use of contraceptives among married couples. As noted earlier, there was also an increase in the average age at first marriage of females, from 18.4 to 19.7 years, during this period. Although most of these changes occurred in the urban areas and among the privileged segment

Table 24. Estimates of total fertility rate by source

United Nations		Statistical Centre		Aghajanian	
Period/year	TFR	Period/year	TFR	Period/year	TFR
1950-1955	7.13				
1955-1960	7.20				
1960-1965	7.26				
1965-1970	6.97	1966	8.4	1966	7.7
1970-1975	6.54				
1975-1980	6.50	1976	5.5	1976	6.3
1980-1985	6.80				
1985-1990	6.00	1986	6.4	1986	7.0
1990-1995	5.30	1991	5.7		
		1992	5.3		
		1993	4.9		

Sources: United Nations, *World Population Prospects: The 1996 Revision;* Statistical Centre of Iran; and Akbar Aghajanian, "Population change in Iran, 1966-1986: A stalled demographic transition", *Population and Development Review,* vol. 17, No. 4 (1994).

of the population, official estimates made by the Statistical Centre indicate a remarkable decline in TFR from 8.4 in 1966 to 5.5 in 1976, representing a reduction of about three children per woman.

The various estimates also point to a significant increase in TFR between 1976 and 1986; according to official estimates, TFR increased from 5.5 to 6.4 children per woman during this period. Analysis also reveals that the increase in marital fertility was most apparent in urban areas, where the greatest fertility decline had occurred between 1966 and 1976. The increase in fertility between 1976 and 1986 is attributed largely to the absence of a national government family planning programme. The post-1979 Islamic Revolutionary Government did not consider population growth a problem, but viewed it as a way to increase the strength of the Moslem nation. Women were exhorted to marry and bear children; the widowed and divorced were urged to remarry. The family planning programme of the previous regime was abandoned, family planning clinics were shut down, and contraceptives became difficult to obtain. Further, abortion and sterilization were declared illegal. This pro-natalist orientation of the post-Revolutionary Government was strengthened by the war with Iraq, which began in September 1980, soon after the revolution, and resulted in heavy casualties.

The decrease in TFR since the second half of the 1980s could largely be attributed to a change in official perception regarding population size and growth. The country's economic conditions began to worsen owing to the effects of economic dislocation and disinvestment during the eight-year war with Iraq, the disastrous effects of the economic embargo, falling prices of oil, flight of capital and exodus of trained personnel. These developments have increasingly weakened the government's ability to provide the expanding population with basic necessities such as food, health care, education and employment. The results of the 1986 census also clearly pointed to the imperative need for moderating the rate of population growth. In 1989, soon after the end of the war, the Islamic Consultative Assembly issued a National Birth Control Policy, and the First

Economic, Social and Cultural Plan of the Islamic Republic of Iran (1989-1993) included a policy to reduce the rate of population growth, increase contraceptive coverage, raise the level of women's education and promote the participation of women in the socio-economic management of the family and society in general.

The important goals of the new family planning programme, announced in December 1989, are to (a) encourage the spacing of birth with three to four years between pregnancies; (b) discourage pregnancies among women below age 18 and over age 35; and (c) limit the total number of children per family to three. Since its creation, the new family planning programme has been gaining political, ideological and economic support. The programme, which now forms an integral part of the health delivery network, provides a wide range of contraceptive methods free or at low cost. There is official encouragement for male and female sterilization. The Islamic regime has also popularized the importance of practising family planning, by means of Friday Sermons and through other media. A 1993 law limits state benefits to a couple's first three children only.

It is clear from discussions in the foregoing paragraphs that family planning has played an important role in determining the levels of fertility in the Islamic Republic of Iran. Data from various surveys indicate that levels of contraceptive knowledge and use have been increasing among Iranian women. According to the 1976/77 Iranian Fertility Survey, about 85 per cent of the women had heard of the oral contraceptive and 35.5 per cent of currently married women were using contraception. The 1992 Contraceptive Prevalence Survey revealed 90 per cent knowledge of at least one contraceptive method and 64.6 per cent use of some type of contraception.

Data from the 1976/77 Survey and the 1992 Survey also showed that contraceptive prevalence was higher among urban compared with rural women, but the rural-urban gap in use that existed in 1976 (33.9 percentage points) had narrowed by 1992 (22.6 percentage points), reflecting a faster increase in the proportion using contraception among rural compared with urban currently married women. The results of the two surveys also show that the proportion of currently married women using contraceptives was higher among the literate than among the illiterate, among the older compared with the younger, and among those with four or more children than among those with three or fewer children (annex table D.1).

According to the 1992 Contraceptive Prevalence Survey, the pill was the most popular method of contraception, with about 23 per cent of all currently married women in the country reportedly using this method. This proportion, however, was significantly higher in rural areas (26.1 per cent) than in urban areas (20.1 per cent), and among illiterate (26.9 per cent) compared with literate (20.3 per cent) women. The traditional method of withdrawal was found to be the second most popular method used by 20 per cent of all currently married women in the country, but being more popular among urban (27.0 per cent) than rural (10.4 per cent) women and among literate (27.7 per cent) compared with illiterate (9.9 per cent) women. Female sterilization or tubectomy was the third most popular method resorted to by around 7.6 per cent of all currently married women in urban as well as rural areas, but being more common among the illiterate (9.5 per cent) than among the literate (5.6 per cent) of the currently married women. The IUD used by 7.1

per cent of all currently married women in the country was remarkably more popular in urban areas (10.0 per cent) than in rural areas (3.1 per cent) and among literate than illiterate women (table 25).

3. Marital disruption

Persons who are widowed or divorced/separated constitute that segment of the population living in a state of marital disruption. As noted earlier in section C, "Women's profile", in 1991 about 6 per cent of females and 1.4 per cent of males aged 10 years and over were reported to be widowed, while the incidence of divorce was very much lower, less than half a per cent among both males and females. It was also noted that the considerably higher incidence of widowhood among females relative to males was due to the higher male than female mortality as well as to the higher rate of remarriage among widowers compared with widows.

In the past, divorce was authorized at the will of the husband in conformity with the Muslim law, and was effected through repudiation of the wife by the husband. The most common form of repudiation was the so-called triple repudiation whereby a husband pronounced the traditional formula "I divorce you" (Talak) three times. However, men's rights to arbitrary

Table 25. Contraceptive prevalence rate and contraceptive method use among currently married women by residence and literacy status: 1992

Residence	Literacy status	Contraceptive prevalence rate (percentage)	Contraceptive prevalence rate of methods (percentage)					
			Pill	Condom	IUD	Vasectomy	Tubectomy	Traditional method
Iran	Total	64.6	22.6	6.4	7.1	0.9	7.6	20.0
	Literate	73.2	20.3	8.4	10.1	1.1	5.6	27.7
	Illiterate	52.6	25.9	3.7	3.1	0.5	9.5	9.9
Urban	Total	74.1	20.1	8.0	10.0	1.3	7.7	27.0
	Literate	77.4	18.3	9.3	11.6	1.4	5.7	31.0
	Illiterate	66.6	24.1	4.8	6.6	1.1	12.8	17.2
Rural	Total	51.6	26.1	4.2	3.1	0.3	7.4	10.4
	Literate	59.7	26.2	5.7	5.4	0.3	5.7	16.7
	Illiterate	48.2	26.5	3.3	2.0	0.3	8.5	7.0

Source: Ministry of Health and Medical Education, *Contraceptive Prevalence Survey, 1992.*

divorce were curbed with the promulgation of the Family Protection Law. This Law also gives a wife increased protection and allows her to initiate divorce proceedings if her husband deserts or mistreats her, or if he takes a second wife without the consent of the first.

In terms of current legislative provisions, a woman can dissolve her marriage in the event she deems that there is a necessity for divorce, through (a) judicial divorce, meaning that a divorce can be obtained through court proceedings; (b) *Khol* divorce, by which the wife may obtain a divorce owing to her repulsion of the husband, ceding property to the husband; or (c) *Mubarat* divorce, which may be sought by the wife or the husband due to mutual repulsion. Amendments to the divorce laws ratified by the Islamic Consultative Assembly in 1992 also make it obligatory on the part of the husband to pay the wife a certain sum of money determined by the court as compensation for her years of household management and upbringing of children.

According to the 1966 census, one in six marriages terminated in divorce, the divorce rate being higher in urban than in rural areas. A 1969 study also reported a divorce rate of one in four marriages in Tehran. However, the incidence of divorce has been declining since the enactment of the Family Protection Law, and data for 1986 and 1991 indicate that the proportion of the divorced among persons aged 10 years and over declined from 0.4 per cent in 1986 to 0.3 per cent in 1991 for males and from 0.6 to 0.4 per cent for females during the same period (see table 10).

E. WOMEN IN ECONOMIC LIFE

1. Background

Historically, Iranian women have taken an active part in various economic activities. In the rural areas, women's participation is evident in several activities related to the agrarian economy, and they perform a significant function in income-generating activities at the household level. In urban areas also, women play important roles in all spheres of economic activity,

with many of them enjoying financial independence, having an important say in household financial matters, and contributing substantially to the economic well-being of their families.

Although the Constitution of the Islamic Republic of Iran attaches great importance to the woman's role as a mother and her significance in maintaining strong family bonds and affectionate relationships, it also considers women's employment and their social and economic activities to be very meaningful and conducive to social well-being. The preamble to the Constitution states: "While retaining their significant and worthy role of motherhood in raising children with ideological beliefs and attitudes, women, alongside men, pioneer and strive for achievement in the active fields of life. Consequently, women enjoy a more valuable and higher moral status from the Islamic point of view". The guidelines on women's employment, ratified by the Supreme Council of the Cultural Revolution, also include policies supporting the promotion of women's active participation in the cultural, social and economic spheres.

The Iranian labour laws have not only taken into consideration the various international recommendations relating to women's employment but also ensure that the rules and regulations framed under these laws are in conformity with the importance that Islam accords to the status of women within the family. Thus, the various labour rules and regulations are so framed as to enable women engaged in employment outside their homes to also assume responsibility for their household tasks.

The current labour laws and regulations prohibit engaging female workers under 18 years of age in strenuous and potentially physically harmful tasks and in night-shift work. These laws also require that pregnant women not be engaged in hard and hazardous occupations without any reduction in remuneration, and that expectant mothers be granted maternity leave with full pay up to three months. The Iranian labour laws also prohibit discrimination based on age, sex, race, nationality, and political and religious beliefs in the matter of determining wages and remuneration, and ensure that men and women receive equal wages for equal work.

2. Labour-force participation

A numerical distribution of the total as well as economically active population aged 10 years and over by sex and residence in 1976, 1986 and 1991 is given in annex table E.1, and the percentage distribution in table 26.

It will be noted that although females have constituted around 49 per cent of the total working-age population (10 years and over) in all three years, they have accounted for only about 10-15 per cent of the country's workforce or economically active population in these years. For instance, in 1991, females constituted only 11.1 per cent of the total economically active persons in the country, the proportion being slightly higher (11.3 per cent) in the urban than in the rural (10.8 per cent) areas.

The small proportionate share of women in the country's labour force is also reflected in their labour-force participation rates (table 27). In 1991, for example, only about 9 per cent of females aged 10 years and over were economically active or in the labour force, the corresponding rate for males being 65.5 per cent. Despite various constitutional and legal provisions favouring women's participation in economic activities, the labour-force participation rate of Iranian women is quite low and is also among the lowest in the world.

Table 26. Percentage distribution of the total and economically active population aged 10 years and over by sex and residence: 1976, 1986 and 1991

Year/sex	Iran		Urban		Rural	
	Total population 10+	Economic-ally active population 10+	Total population 10+	Economic-ally active population 10+	Total population 10+	Economic-ally active population 10+
1976						
Both sexes	100.0	100.0	100.0	100.0	100.0	100.0
Male	51.3	85.2	52.7	88.7	49.9	82.4
Female	48.7	14.8	47.3	11.3	50.1	17.6
1986						
Both sexes	100.0	100.0	100.0	100.0	100.0	100.0
Male	51.2	89.8	51.5	89.4	50.9	90.2
Female	48.8	10.2	48.5	10.6	49.1	9.8
1991						
Both sexes	100.0	100.0	100.0	100.0	100.0	100.0
Male	51.7	88.9	51.9	88.7	51.5	89.2
Female	48.3	11.1	48.1	11.3	48.5	10.8

Source: Statistical Centre of Iran.

Table 27. Labour-force participation rates of the population aged 10 years and over by sex and residence: 1976, 1986 and 1991

(Percentage)

Year	Iran			Urban			Rural		
	Both sexes	Male	Female	Both sexes	Male	Female	Both sexes	Male	Female
1976	42.5	70.8	12.9	37.9	63.9	9.0	47.2	77.9	16.6
1986	39.0	68.4	8.2	38.4	66.8	8.4	39.7	70.3	7.9
1991	38.1	65.5	8.7	37.8	64.6	8.9	38.6	66.9	8.6

Source: Statistical Centre of Iran.

The very low labour-force participation rates reported in respect of Iranian women by successive national censuses is largely due to the gross under-reporting of female economic activity in these censuses. In the first instance, the conventional definitions employed by the censuses to measure the extent of people's participation in the labour force do not recognize most of the activities usually performed by women. In the Islamic Republic of Iran, as in several other countries in the Asian and Pacific region, activities such as fuel and water collection, home gardening, and livestock and poultry rearing, which are almost exclusively performed by women and are economically valuable, are not covered by the definitions and concepts of the economically active persons adopted by the country's censuses. Further, since women largely combine their economic activities with household duties, there has been a tendency to overlook their significant contribution to economic production and to classify them simply as housewives on the basis of their involvement in domestic chores.

Another factor contributing to the under-reporting of rural women's labour-force participation is the reluctance of male household heads to acknowledge the economic activities of their wives and daughters outside the household. This is particularly true in those countries in which the Islamic custom of purdah inhibits the employment of women. Several studies have also reported that where the enumerator as well as the respondent are males, there is often a tendency to under-report the economic activities of women. Further, it is likely that in responding to the relevant census questions, women themselves may regard their unpaid activities in family farms or other household enterprises as not constituting economic activity.

It will also be noted from annex table E.1 and text tables 26 and 27 that there was a decrease in female participation in economic activity in absolute as well as relative terms between 1976 and 1986. For the country as a whole, the number of females reported as being economically active declined by 141,094 from 1,449,006 in 1976 to 1,307,912 in 1986. This decline was due to a very sharp decline in the number of economically active females in

rural areas from 959,708 to 561,903, or by 397,805; in the urban areas, the number of economically active females had increased by 252,020 during the same period.

Available data also indicate that the decline in the number of economically active females between 1976 and 1986 had occurred at ages 10-24 and 30-54 years, but was particularly marked at ages 10-14 and 15-19 years (annex table E.2). The decrease in the number of economically active females at the younger age groups was largely due to the increasing participation of rural girls in the education system. As noted earlier, enrolment of girls in primary and secondary education levels increased rapidly between 1976 and 1986 (tables 11 and 12). The fall in the number of economically active females at ages 20-24 years was also partly due to the desire of married women at these ages to stay at home to take care of their newly born children.

It must also be noted that after the cultural revolution there was a severe deterioration in the employment situation throughout the country. Several factors, such as the departure of factory owners, sequestrations, continuing rural-to-urban migration, and the displacement of the people by the war with Iraq contributed to severe unemployment in the country. In a situation of job shortages, socio-cultural norms favour the employment of males over females. Further, during the war with Iraq, investments were fashioned to suit the country's defence objectives, and the employment opportunities created as a result required employing more males than females.

The decrease in the number of economically active females between 1976 and 1986 is also reflected in the trends in age-specific labour-force participation rates. During this 10-year period, there was a decline in female labour-force participation rates at all ages, but this decline was more marked at ages 10-14, 15-19 and 20-24 years. Since 1986, there has been an increase in female labour-force participation rates at all ages except at ages 10-14 years, reflecting the increasing enrolment of girls in elementary education (table 28).

Table 28. Female age-specific labour-force participation rates: 1976, 1986 and 1991

Age group	1976	1986	1991
10-14	10.7	4.5	3.9
15-19	15.7	9.4	11.1
20-24	17.9	12.0	14.0
25-29	16.1	11.1	11.5
30-34	14.1	11.2	11.2
35-39	12.8	9.5	10.8
40-44	11.7	7.8	8.8
45.49	10.9	6.2	6.8
50-54	9.7	5.4	5.0
55-59	8.1	4.8	4.1
60-64	6.6	4.2	3.7
65+	4.5	2.8	3.5
All ages	13.4	9.0	9.9

Source: Statistical Centre of Iran.

3. Labour-force characteristics

(a) Activities status

In terms of the standard definition, the economically active persons, or those in the labour force, comprise two categories:

(i) Employed persons, or those who during the reference period were either working for pay or profit in cash or kind, or had a job but were not at work owing to absence on leave, illness, strike or other reasons;

(ii) Unemployed persons, or those who, during the reference period, were without work but were currently available for work and seeking work, in that they had taken specific steps during a specified recent period to seek employment, either as paid employees or as self-employed.

The numerical distribution of the economically active males and females by activity or labour-force status and residence for the years 1976, 1986 and 1991 is given in annex table E.3, and the percentage distribution in table 29. It will be noted from table 29 that the proportion of the labour force that is employed is significantly higher among males, while the proportion unemployed is significantly higher among females. In 1991, for instance, nearly a quarter (24.4 per cent) of the female labour force was reported to be unemployed, compared with less than a tenth (9.5 per cent) of the male labour force. Thus, the proportion of the working-age females actually in the labour force and that of the female labour force that is employed are considerably lower than the respective proportions among males.

It is also evident from table 29 that the unemployment rate or proportion of the economically active persons reported as unemployed was higher in the rural compared with the

Table 29. Percentage distribution of economically active persons aged 10 years and over by activity status, sex and residence: 1976, 1986 and 1991

Year/activity status	Iran			Urban			Rural		
	Both sexes	Male	Female	Both sexes	Male	Female	Both sexes	Male	Female
1976									
All active persons	100.0	100.0	100.0	100.0	100.0	100.0	100.0	100.0	100.0
Employed	89.8	90.9	83.6	94.9	95.0	94.0	85.8	87.4	78.4
Unemployed	10.2	9.1	16.4	5.1	5.0	6.0	14.2	12.6	21.6
1986									
All active persons	100.0	100.0	100.0	100.0	100.0	100.0	100.0	100.0	100.0
Employed	85.8	87.1	74.6	84.7	86.4	70.8	89.6	91.1	78.5
Unemployed	14.2	12.9	25.4	15.3	13.6	29.2	10.4	8.9	21.5
1991									
All active persons	100.0	100.0	100.0	100.0	100.0	100.0	100.0	100.0	100.0
Employed	88.9	90.5	75.6	89.6	91.1	78.5	87.9	89.8	71.7
Unemployed	11.1	9.5	24.4	10.4	8.9	21.5	12.1	10.2	28.3

Source: Statistical Centre of Iran.

urban areas in 1976 and in 1991, while in 1986 the urban unemployment rates were significantly higher than the rural rates. In 1991, the rural female unemployment rate of 28.3 per cent was nearly seven percentage points higher than the urban rate of 21.5 per cent.

The overall unemployment rates also mask the marked variations in these rates among various age groups. Available data indicate that unemployment has always been a more serious problem for the young and for the elderly females. In 1991, for instance, more than a third of the female labour force at ages 10-24 years and 65 years and over were reported to be unemployed, the unemployment rate being as high as 43 per cent among females aged 10-14 years and 46 per cent among those aged 15-19 years (table 30 and annex table E.4).

(b) Industrial attachment

The numerical distribution of the employed males and females by industry (or the activity of the establishment in which they worked in 1986 and 1991) is given in annex table E.5.

The percentage distribution by industry of employed females in 1976, 1986 and 1991 and that of employed males in 1986 and 1991 is given in table 31.

It will be noted from table 31 that there were considerable shifts in the industrial attachment pattern of employed females between 1976 and 1991. In 1976, nearly 53 per cent of all employed females were concentrated in the manufacturing sector, another about 24 per cent in community, social and personal services, and a further about 19 per cent in the agriculture and allied industrial sector. This pattern had changed over the next 10 years with a dramatic decline in the proportion of employed females engaged in manufacturing to 21-6 per cent and an equally dramatic increase in the proportion engaged in community, social and personal services, to 42.4 per cent, while the proportion among employed females working in agriculture and allied industries had also increased significantly to 26.6 per cent by 1986. In other words, in 1986, the most important source of employment for females was the service sector, followed by the agricultural sector, and thereafter by the manufacturing sector.

Table 30. Age-specific employment[a/] and unemployment rates[b/] of the female labour force: 1976, 1986 and 1991

(Percentage)

Age group	1976		1986		1991	
	Employment rate	Unemployment rate	Employment rate	Unemployment rate	Employment rate	Unemployment rate
10-14	87.7	12.3	56.7	43.3	57.1	42.9
15-19	83.6	16.4	53.0	47.0	53.9	46.1
20-24	85.6	14.4	61.9	38.1	67.1	32.9
25-29	86.5	13.5	84.3	15.7	84.1	15.9
30-34	84.5	15.5	93.4	6.6	93.2	6.8
35-39	80.2	19.8	95.0	5.0	96.3	3.7
40-44	77.7	22.3	95.0	5.0	96.6	3.4
45-49	76.0	24.0	94.2	5.8	95.9	4.1
50-54	77.3	22.7	92.2	7.8	93.2	6.7
55-59	77.3	22.7	89.7	10.3	90.2	9.8
60-64	82.0	18.0	85.2	14.8	82.0	18.0
65+	82.8	17.2	67.9	32.1	64.6	35.4
All ages 10+	83.6	16.4	74.6	25.4	75.6	24.4

Source: Statistical Centre of Iran.

[a/] Employment rate is the number employed as a percentage of total economically active persons or labour force.

[b/] Unemployment rate is the number unemployed as a percentage of total economically active persons or labour force.

Table 31. Percentage distribution of employed persons aged 10 years and over by major industrial sector and sex: 1976, 1986 and 1991

Major industrial sector	1976	1986		1991	
	Female	Male	Female	Male	Female
Agriculture, forestry, hunting and fishing	18.8	29.2	26.6	25.7	12.9
Mining and quarrying	0.3	0.3	0.1	0.8	0.2
Manufacturing	52.7	12.4	21.6	14.4	24.6
Electricity, gas and water	0.6	0.9	0.2	1.1	0.3
Construction	0.2	12.0	1.0	11.5	0.7
Trade, hotel and restaurant	1.0	8.6	1.5	10.3	1.3
Transport, storage and communication	0.7	6.2	0.9	6.3	0.9
Finance, insurance and business	0.9	1.0	1.1	1.5	1.3
Community, social and personal services	23.6	26.3	42.4	24.5	49.5
Activities not adequately defined	1.2	3.1	4.6	3.9	8.3
Total	100.0	100.0	100.0	100.0	100.0

Source: Statistical Centre of Iran.

The drastic reduction in the proportion among employed females engaged in the manufacturing sector was due to several factors. First, as noted earlier, many factories that had earlier employed a large number of women were closed down with the departure of their owners after the cultural revolution. Further, the relatively low skill levels of women and the higher welfare costs involved in their employment were also important factors that discouraged employers from recruiting females in a situation of increasing unemployment. However, since 1986, there has been an increase in the proportion among employed females absorbed in the service and manufacturing sectors and a decrease in their proportion in the agricultural sector, resulting in the service sector being the most important sector of employment for women, followed by the manufacturing sector and the agricultural sector.

The pattern of industrial attachment also varies between the urban and rural areas. In 1986, for instance, the largest proportion among employed females was engaged in the service sector (71.9 per cent) in the urban areas, and in the agriculture and allied industrial sector (54.5 per cent) in rural areas, while the manufacturing sector was the second most important source of employment for women in the urban (11.8 per cent) and rural (33.2 per cent) areas. But in 1991, while the pattern of industrial attachment of urban employed women remained

unchanged, in the rural areas the importance of the agricultural sector as an avenue for female employment appears to have diminished and that of the manufacturing sector to have increased; about 44 per cent of all employed females were engaged in the manufacturing sector and only 32 per cent in the agricultural sector (table 32).

The diminishing importance of the agricultural sector and the rising importance of the manufacturing sector as employment avenues for rural females can be partly explained by the increasing school attendance of rural girls and unwillingness on the part of educated girls to perform manual work in the agricultural sector, as well as their preference for jobs in the manufacturing sector. Nevertheless, it is hard to accept that there was actually a decrease in the number of rural women employed in the agricultural sector by 100,000 between 1986 and 1991 when the number of rural females of working age (10 years and over) had increased by over 639,000 during the same five-year period. Since it is well known that a very large number of rural women participate in almost all agricultural activities, it is likely that the reported decrease in the number and relative share of rural employed females engaged in the agricultural sector could be due to the reluctance on the part of the male household heads or respondents to acknowledge openly the economic contribution of their wives and daughters.

Table 32. Percentage distribution of employed women aged 10 years and over by major industrial sector and residence: 1976, 1986 and 1991

Major industrial sector	1976		1986		1991	
	Urban	Rural	Urban	Rural	Urban	Rural
Agriculture, forestry, hunting and fishing	2.4	28.9	2.4	54.5	1.2	31.5
Mining and quarrying	0.6	0.1	0.1	0.1	0.4	0.0
Manufacturing	31.2	65.9	11.8	33.2	12.3	44.2
Electricity, gas and water	1.1	0.4	0.4	0.1	0.4	0.0
Construction	0.4	0.0	1.1	0.8	0.8	0.5
Trade, hotel and restaurant	2.2	0.3	2.4	0.4	2.0	0.4
Transport, storage and communication	1.8	0.0	1.4	0.2	1.4	0.2
Finance, insurance and business	2.0	0.0	2.0	0.0	2.0	0.0
Community, social and personal services	56.2	3.6	71.8	8.3	73.6	11.7
Activities not adequately defined	2.0	0.8	6.6	2.4	5.9	11.4
Total	100.0	100.0	100.0	100.0	100.0	100.0

Source: Statistical Centre of Iran.

(c) Occupational structure

The occupational structure, or the distribution of employed persons by the kind of work performed during the reference period, is shown in annex table E.6 and table 33.

The occupational structure of employed females more or less reflects their industrial attachment pattern. In 1986 and 1991, the largest proportion of employed females were engaged as professional, technical and related workers, and the proportion in this category has been increasing steadily, from 15.5 per cent in 1976 to 35.2 per cent in 1986, and to 42.5 per cent in 1991. Available data, not shown in the tables, also indicate that 77.3 per cent of female workers in this category work as teachers, and another 15.1 per cent as physicians, nurses and paramedical personnel. The second largest proportion of employed females were engaged as agricultural and allied workers in 1976 and 1986, but as production, transport, equipment operators and labourers in 1991. Between 1986 and 1991, there was a decline in female agricultural workers in both absolute and relative terms. The proportions among female workers engaged in clerical and related occupations also increased substantially between 1986 and 1991.

Table 33. Percentage distribution of employed persons aged 10 years and over by major occupational category and sex: 1976, 1986 and 1991

Major occupational category	1976	1986		1991	
	Female	Male	Female	Male	Female
Professional, technical and related workers	15.5	7.1	35.2	8.8	42.5
Administrative and managerial workers	0.1	0.4	0.1	0.6	0.1
Clerical and related workers	5.2	3.2	4.8	5.3	7.0
Sales workers	0.6	7.5	1.2	10.0	1.2
Service workers	5.6	4.2	3.3	4.7	3.0
Agriculture and allied workers	18.7	29.8	26.6	25.9	13.0
Production, transport, equipment operators and labourers	52.9	34.0	23.1	35.5	25.1
Workers not classifiable	1.4	13.8	5.7	9.2	8.0
All occupation	100.0	100.0	100.0	100.0	100.0

Source: Statistical Centre of Iran.

(d) Employment status

The employed persons have been classified according to their employment status into four broad categories: employers; wage and salaried workers or employees; own-account workers or self-employed; and unpaid family workers.

It is clear from annex table E.7 and table 34 that the majority of the employed, among both males and females, are wage and salaried workers; in 1991, about 60 per cent of employed females and 50.2 per cent of employed males belonged to this employment status category. The high proportion of wage and salaried workers reflects the extent of organized economic activity in the country. Available data also indicate a significant increase, in absolute as well as relative terms, in wage and salaried employees between 1986 and 1991, and this increase was more marked in the case of employed females compared with employed males. It is also evident from the tables that the proportion of wage and salaried workers is considerably higher in the public sector than in the private sector. In 1991, nearly 50 per cent of all employed females were working as wage and salaried employers in the public sector and 9.6 per cent in the private sector, the corresponding proportions for males being 31.4 and 18.8 per cent.

Own-account workers or the self-employed constituted the second largest proportion among employed males and females in 1986 as well as

in 1991, the proportion for males being more than twice that for females. Although there was a decline in the number as well as relative share of unpaid family workers between 1986 and 1991, nearly 12 per cent of all employed females were reported to be engaged as unpaid family workers in 1991, compared with 1.6 per cent among employed males. A considerably higher proportion among employed males (3.3 per cent) than among employed females (0.8 per cent) were employers, and there was a decline in the number of female employers from 13,719 in 1986 to 9,647 in 1991.

F. WOMEN IN PUBLIC LIFE

1. The political scene

The active participation of Iranian women in political processes was prominently displayed in the 1970s and 1980s when their presence in the political scene and their impact on the events of the day were tremendous, despite their lack of previous experience in political activities. Women's endeavours during the Islamic Revolution of the 1970s were an exemplification of a mass movement based on religious and social values. It has generally been acknowledged that women's active participation was vital to the success of the Revolution, and that their dynamic efforts and presence resulted in positive and profound changes in the social, cultural and moral aspects of Iranian society.

Table 34. Percentage distribution of employed persons aged 10 years and over by employment status and sex: 1986 and 1991

Employment status	1986		1991	
	Male	Female	Male	Female
Employer	3.3	1.4	3.3	0.8
Own-account worker	42.0	18.3	43.8	20.8
Wage/salaried worker	48.1	51.8	50.2	59.5
Private sector	*17.7*	*10.0*	*18.8*	*9.6*
Public sector	*30.4*	*41.8*	*31.4*	*49.9*
Unpaid family worker	2.7	21.5	1.6	12.0
Status not reported	3.9	7.0	1.1	6.9
All statuses	100.0	100.0	100.0	100.0

Source: Statistical Centre of Iran.

Women's participation en masse in the country's political life was also very prominent and significant during the eight-year war with Iraq. The women's mobilization units set up in mosques, government departments and factories rendered valuable service behind the front line in preparatory and supportive tasks. The tireless efforts of these units in exhorting the people to take part directly or indirectly in the defence of the country and to make personal sacrifices and practise austerity, and in mobilizing much-needed financial resources, helped to a considerable extent in defeating the foreign forces. Even today, those women's units are actively engaged in the nation's reconstruction efforts and in implementing various socio-economic development programmes.

The years following the end of the war with Iraq witnessed a significant increase in women's participation in political activities such as the national elections, demonstrations to support or oppose certain issues, and in group meetings and associations, as well as in their role in the decision-making processes at various levels. This increased participation has largely been due to the efforts of various governmental and non-governmental organizations engaged in women's development as well as the active support of the government. The Constitution of the Islamic Republic of Iran enacted in 1980 guarantees women equal rights to those of men in regard to participation in the political process, as both voters and candidates. Almost all rules and regulations that had discriminated against women had been nullified.

Over the years, an increasing number of Iranian women have exercised their voting rights at the referendum, presidential elections and parliamentary elections. Available data indicate that in the presidential elections held in 1992, for instance, women constituted 44 per cent of all voters. However, despite the fact that an increasing number of women have been nominated as candidates and an increasing percentage of eligible women have voted at successive elections, women continue to be underrepresented in the Islamic Consultative Assembly or Parliament. The number of women parliamentarians increased from four in the first parliament to nine in the fourth parliament, but women constitute only 3.3 per cent of the total number (277) of parliamentarians.

It must, however, be noted that key positions in planning and policy-making areas have been made available to women. For example, women representatives in parliament serve as members of important parliamentary committees. In addition, several women have been appointed as counsellors to ministers.

2. Public service

Available data indicate that the number of females employed in the public sector doubled between 1981 and 1991, and that of the 1.968 million public sector employees in 1994, nearly 603,000, or about 31 per cent, were females. The substantial rise in the number of females employed in the public sector reflects the importance that the Iranian government attaches to the role of women in public administration.

The proportionate share of females in total employees varies between ministries, ranging from less than 5 per cent in ministries that are engaged in technical and industrial activities (e.g. Ministry of Mines and Metals, Ministry of Oil, Ministry of Energy, and Ministry of Heavy Industries) to more than 40 per cent in those ministries engaged in social development, such as the Ministry of Health (40 per cent) and the Ministry of Education (43.8 per cent). In the Ministries of Health and of Education, women are mostly engaged in the traditional fields of teaching, nursing and other health-related jobs.

In 1994, about 34 per cent of all female public sector employees were college graduates, the corresponding proportion being 19.5 per cent in 1978. In this connection, it may be noted that the policy of the government has been to encourage women with college education and specialist qualifications to assume management and executive responsibilities in order to utilize their capabilities in high level-positions.

An important feature of female employment in the public sector is that only a very small proportion (about 5 per cent) are in high-level management and decision-making positions. At present, the highest official position held by an Iranian woman is that of Adviser to the President on Women's Affairs, established in 1992 within the President's Office. However, the number of women holding general management positions in government ministries/departments has been increasing steadily over the years, resulting in 342 women being placed in management posts in 1994. There has also been a rise in the number of women in middle-level management positions, and at present several women are employed at this level throughout the country. The increasing appointment of women to decision-making positions has largely been due to the increased emphasis of government authorities on integrating women's potential into economic development as well as to the active efforts of various organizations in promoting the advancement of women.

The increasing presence of women at higher decision-making levels has largely facilitated the planning and implementation of policies and programmes for enhancing the status of women in the country. In this respect, it must be noted that another important decision-making institution is the Women's Social and Cultural Council, comprising 15 qualified professionals responsible for preparing comprehensive proposals that would enable the formulation of appropriate policies to improve the social and cultural status of women in the country.

Although females are guaranteed equal rights to those of males, several occupations explicitly restrict the employment of women. For example, women are not appointed as judges or recruited into the armed forces. In recent years, however, women have been serving as advisers to the courts of law, and at present there are 185 registered female attorneys-at-law who offer legal advice. Similarly, while women were not recruited as police officers, a number of women have been serving in the police department in administrative and clerical positions, and many duties continue to be handled by women in the passport and traffic divisions. Recently, the Islamic Consultative Assembly ratified certain provisions for the employment of women in the police and armed forces.

PART II
ANNEX TABLES

Table C.1 Numerical distribution of the enumerated population by sex and province: 1986 and 1991

Province	1986			1991		
	Both sexes	Male	Female	Both sexes	Male	Female
Tehran	8 712	4 475	4 237	9 982	5 171	4 811
Markazi	1 082	550	532	1 183	610	573
Gilan	2 081	1 054	1 027	2 204	1 125	1 079
Mazandaran	3 419	1 723	1 696	3 794	1 937	1 857
East Azarbayejan	4 114	2 106	2 008	4 420	2 282	2 138
West Azarbayejan	1 972	1 002	970	2 285	1 170	1 115
Kermanshahan	1 463	754	709	1 623	847	776
Khugestan	2 681	1 372	1 309	3 176	1 631	1 545
Fars	3 194	1 635	1 559	3 544	1 826	1 718
Kerman	1 623	822	801	1 863	953	910
Khorasan	5 281	2 683	2 598	6 013	3 076	2 937
Esfahan	3 295	1 705	1 590	3 682	1 912	1 770
Sistan and Baluchestan	1 197	603	594	1 455	741	714
Kordestan	1 078	552	526	1 233	636	597
Hamadan	1 506	784	722	1 652	859	793
Chaharmahal and Bakhitiyari	631	324	307	747	387	360
Lorestan	1 367	702	665	1 501	774	727
Ilam	382	198	184	441	227	214
Kohkiloyeh and Boyer Ahmad	412	213	199	496	256	240
Bushehr	612	311	301	694	359	335
Zanjan	1 589	811	778	1 776	915	861
Semnan	417	214	203	458	235	223
Yazd	574	297	277	691	362	329
Hormozgan	762	389	373	925	477	448
Islamic Republic of Iran	49 445	25 281	24 164	55 837	28 768	27 069

Source: Statistical Centre of Iran, *A Statistical Reflection of the Islamic Republic of Iran,* Nos. 9 and 12.

Table C.2 Indicators of gender balance by province: 1986 and 1991

Province	1986			1991		
	Percent-age female	Males per 100 females	Females per 100 males	Percent-age female	Males per 100 females	Females per 100 males
Tehran	48.6	105.6	94.7	48.2	107.5	93.0
Markazi	49.1	103.5	96.6	48.4	106.5	93.9
Gilan	49.4	102.6	97.5	49.0	104.3	95.9
Mazandaran	49.6	101.6	98.5	49.0	104.3	95.9
East Azarbayejan	48.8	104.9	95.3	48.4	106.7	93.7
West Azarbayejan	49.2	103.3	96.8	48.8	104.9	95.3
Kermanshahan	48.5	106.3	94.0	47.8	109.2	91.6
Khugestan	48.8	104.8	95.4	48.6	105.6	94.7
Fars	48.8	105.0	95.3	48.5	106.3	94.1
Kerman	49.3	102.7	97.3	48.8	104.7	95.5
Khorasan	49.2	103.3	96.8	48.8	104.7	95.5
Esfahan	48.3	107.2	93.3	48.1	108.0	92.6
Sistan and Baluchestan	49.6	101.5	98.5	49.1	103.8	96.4
Kordestan	48.8	105.0	95.2	48.4	106.5	93.9
Hamadan	47.9	108.6	92.1	48.0	108.3	92.3
Chaharmahal and Bakhitiyari	48.7	105.4	94.9	48.2	107.5	93.0
Lorestan	48.6	105.6	94.7	48.4	106.5	93.9
Ilam	48.2	107.5	93.0	48.5	106.1	94.3
Kohkiloyeh and Boyer Ahmad	48.4	107.0	93.4	48.4	106.7	93.8
Bushehr	49.2	103.3	96.8	48.3	107.2	93.3
Zanjan	48.9	104.4	95.8	48.5	106.3	94.1
Semnan	48.7	105.4	94.9	48.7	105.4	95.0
Yazd	48.3	107.2	93.3	47.6	110.0	90.9
Hormozgan	49.0	104.3	95.9	48.5	106.5	93.9
Islamic Republic of Iran	48.9	104.6	95.5	48.5	106.3	94.1

Source: Statistical Centre of Iran.

Table C.3 Numerical distribution of the population by age group and sex: 1986 and 1991

Age group	1986			1991		
	Both sexes	Male	Female	Both sexes	Male	Female
0-4	9 044 823	4 595 958	4 448 865	8 141 285	4 156 291	3 984 994
5-9	7 525 894	3 843 585	3 682 309	9 035 458	4 612 149	4 423 309
10-14	5 903 300	3 053 633	2 849 667	7 547 131	3 901 458	3 645 673
15-19	5 192 202	2 660 364	2 531 838	5 908 903	3 057 609	2 851 294
20-24	4 193 724	2 103 615	2 090 109	4 947 260	2 520 312	2 426 948
25-29	3 652 297	1 839 639	1 812 658	4 005 278	2 012 493	1 992 785
30-34	2 927 983	1 481 475	1 446 508	3 504 220	1 779 932	1 724 288
35-39	2 117 211	1 043 813	1 073 398	2 866 669	1 462 338	1 404 331
40-44	1 655 351	833 703	821 648	2 037 477	1 027 459	1 010 018
45-49	1 585 398	819 225	766 173	1 577 983	798 299	779 684
50-54	1 599 018	856 740	742 278	1 570 622	821 599	749 023
55-59	1 337 746	715 428	622 318	1 442 929	793 283	649 646
60-64	1 184 632	651 864	532 768	1 303 390	723 318	580 072
65+	1 501 718	767 916	733 802	1 890 193	1 065 753	824 440
Age not stated	23 713	14 003	9 710	58 365	36 157	22 208
All ages	49 445 010	25 280 961	24 164 049	55 837 163	28 768 450	27 068 713

Source: Statistical Centre of Iran.

Table C.4 Percentage distribution of the population by five-year age group and sex: 1986 and 1991

Age group	1986			1991		
	Both sexes	Male	Female	Both sexes	Male	Female
0-4	18.3	18.2	18.4	14.6	14.4	14.7
5-9	15.2	15.2	15.3	16.2	16.0	16.3
10-14	11.9	12.1	11.8	13.5	13.6	13.4
15-19	10.5	10.5	10.5	10.6	10.6	10.5
20-24	8.5	8.3	8.6	8.9	8.8	9.0
25-29	7.4	7.3	7.5	7.2	7.0	7.4
30-34	5.9	5.9	5.9	6.3	6.2	6.4
35-39	4.3	4.1	4.4	5.1	5.1	5.2
40-44	3.3	3.3	3.4	3.6	3.6	3.7
45-49	3.2	3.2	3.2	2.8	2.8	2.9
50-54	3.2	3.4	3.1	2.8	2.9	2.8
55-59	2.7	2.8	2.6	2.6	2.8	2.4
60-64	2.4	2.6	2.2	2.3	2.5	2.1
65+[a]	3.1	3.1	3.1	3.5	3.8	3.2
Total	100.0	100.0	100.0	100.0	100.0	100.0

Source: Statistical Centre of Iran.

[a] Including "age not stated".

Table C.5 Total and literate population aged six years and over by sex and residence: 1976, 1986 and 1991

Year/residence	Total population six years and over			Literate population six years and over		
	Both sexes	Male	Female	Both sexes	Male	Female
1976						
Iran	27 112 844	13 925 591	13 187 253	12 877 075	8 197 987	4 679 088
Urban[a/]	13 182 568	6 919 468	6 263 100	8 628 239	5 145 393	3 482 846
Rural[a/]	13 930 276	7 006 123	6 924 153	4 248 836	3 052 294	1 196 242
1986						
Iran	38 708 879	19 822 155	18 886 724	23 913 195	14 077 896	9 835 299
Urban[a/]	21 210 303	10 906 676	10 303 627	15 506 666	8 764 725	6 741 941
Rural[a/]	17 306 861	8 818 371	8 488 490	8 370 643	5 286 753	3 083 890
1991						
Iran	45 855 787	23 675 027	22 180 760	33 966 234	19 091 482	14 874 752
Urban[a/]	26 521 349	13 726 658	12 794 691	21 725 327	11 903 280	9 822 047
Rural[a/]	19 046 594	9 798 949	9 247 645	12 128 006	7 113 652	5 014 354

Source: Statistical Centre of Iran.

[a/] Excluding the unsettled population.

Table D.1 Determinants of current contraceptive use among currently married women: 1976 and 1992

Variable	Percentage currently using contraception	
	1976	1992
Place of residence		
Urban	53.8	74.1
Rural	19.9	51.5
Women's literacy		
Literacy	40.4	73.2
Illiterate	25.3	52.6
Age at time of survey		
15-19 years	16.5	34.4
20-34 years	31.4	64.4
35+ years	41.4	70.9
Number of living children		
Nationwide		
3 or fewer children	31.2	56.9
4 or more children	41.1	72.5
Urban		
3 or fewer children	49.8	69.6
4 or more children	56.1	81.0
Rural		
3 or fewer children	10.4	39.3
4 or more children	27.9	60.8
All currently married women	35.9	64.6

Source: Iranian Fertility Survey, 1976/77 and Contraceptive Prevalence Survey, 1992, cited in Akbar Aghajanian, "A new direction in population policy and family planning in the Islamic Republic of Iran", *Asia-Pacific Population Journal*, vol. 10, No. 1 (1995).

Table E.1 Total population and economically active population aged 10 years and over by sex and residence: 1976, 1986 and 1991

Year and sex	Iran[a/]		Urban		Rural	
	Population 10 years and over		Population 10 years and over		Population 10 years and over	
	Total	Econo-mically active	Total	Econo-mically active	Total	Econo-mically active
1976						
Both sexes	23 002 499	9 796 056	11 427 977	4 335 564	11 574 522	5 460 492
Male	11 796 414	8 347 050	6 017 794	3 846 266	5 778 620	4 500 784
Female	11 206 085	1 449 006	5 410 183	489 298	5 795 902	959 708
1986						
Both sexes	32 870 363	12 820 272	18 279 256	7 025 996	14 435 491	5 727 067
Male	16 839 388	11 512 368	9 410 813	6 284 683	7 349 492	5 165 164
Female	16 030 975	1 307 912	8 868 443	741 313	7 085 999	561 903
1991						
Both sexes	38 655 049	14 736 704	22 483 337	8 488 622	15 934 173	6 150 405
Male	19 997 274	13 107 062	11 664 532	7 530 080	8 208 764	5 488 869
Female	18 657 775	1 629 642	10 818 805	958 542	7 725 409	661 536

Source: Statistical Centre of Iran.

[a/] Figures for the country as a whole include urban, rural and unsettled areas.

Table E.2 Numerical distribution of total and economically active females aged 10 years and over by five-year age group: 1976, 1986 and 1991

Age group	1976		1986		1991	
	Total popula-tion	Econo-mically active popula-tion	Total popula-tion	Econo-mically active popula-tion	Total popula-ion	Econo-mically active popula-tion
10-14	2 044 484	219 713	2 849 667	127 904	3 645 673	142 125
15-19	1 781 726	280 419	2 531 838	237 943	2 851 294	316 609
20-24	1 451 357	259 852	2 090 109	250 972	2 426 948	339 912
25-29	1 101 390	177 479	1 812 658	202 065	1 992 785	229 155
30-34	864 544	122 238	1 446 508	161 478	1 724 288	192 490
35-39	801 279	102 189	1 073 398	101 581	1 404 331	152 161
40-44	773 489	90 642	821 648	64 013	1 010 018	88 824
45-49	638 439	69 554	766 173	47 605	779 684	53 302
50-54	597 376	58 106	742 278	40 415	749 023	37 139
55-59	307 182	24 897	622 318	30 126	649 646	26 844
60-64	282 742	18 711	532 768	22 611	580 072	21 743
65 and over	562 077	25 206	733 802	20 579	824 440	28 441
Not reported	–	–	9 710	620	19 573	897
Total	11 206 085	1 449 006	16 032 875	1 307 912	18 657 775	1 629 642

Source: Statistical Centre of Iran.

Table E.3 Economically active persons aged 10 years and over by activity status, sex and residence: 1976, 1986 and 1991

Year/activity status	Iran[a/]		Urban		Rural	
	Male	Female	Male	Female	Male	Female
1976						
All active persons	8 347 050	1 449 006	3 846 266	489 298	4 500 784	959 708
Employed	7 587 400	1 212 020	3 652 629	460 007	3 934 771	752 013
Unemployed	759 650	236 986	193 637	29 291	566 013	207 695
1986						
All active persons	11 512 368	1 307 912	6 284 683	741 313	5 165 164	561 903
Employed	10 026 230	975 310	5 428 176	524 846	4 541 239	446 258
Unemployed	1 486 138	332 602	856 507	216 467	623 925	115 645
1991						
All active persons	13 107 062	1 629 642	7 530 080	958 542	5 488 869	661 536
Employed	11 865 389	1 231 223	6 856 868	752 010	4 930 587	474 003
Unemployed	1 241 673	398 419	673 212	206 532	558 282	187 533

Source: Statistical Centre of Iran.

[a/] The country totals also include relevant figures for unsettled areas not included in the table.

Table E.4 Numerical distribution of economically active females aged 10 years and over by activity status and five-year age group: 1976, 1986 and 1991

Age group	1976			1986			1991		
	Economically active females			Economically active females			Economically active females		
	Total	Employed	Unemployed	Total	Employed	Unemployed	Total	Employed	Unemployed
10-14	219 713	192 694	27 019	127 904	72 541	55 363	142 125	81 138	60 987
15-19	280 419	234 527	45 892	237 943	126 031	111 912	316 609	170 598	146 011
20-24	259 852	222 390	37 462	250 972	155 400	95 572	339 912	228 220	111 692
25-29	177 479	153 582	23 897	202 065	170 386	31 679	229 155	192 665	36 490
30-34	122 238	103 273	18 965	161 478	150 846	10 632	192 490	179 437	13 053
35-39	102 189	81 932	20 257	101 581	96 531	5 050	152 161	146 606	5 555
40-44	90 642	70 389	20 253	64 013	60 818	3 195	88 824	85 762	3 062
45-49	69 554	52 849	16 705	47 605	44 827	2 778	53 302	51 106	2 196
50-54	58 106	44 915	13 191	40 415	37 263	3 152	37 139	34 643	2 496
55-59	24 897	19 250	5 647	30 126	27 023	3 103	26 844	24 220	2 624
60-64	18 711	15 341	3 370	22 611	19 274	3 337	21 743	17 827	3 916
65 and over	25 206	20 878	4 328	20 579	13 975	6 604	28 441	18 364	10 077
Not reported	–	–	–	620	395	225	897	637	260
All ages 10+	1 449 006	1 212 020	236 986	1 307 912	975 310	332 602	1 629 642	1 231 223	398 419

Source: Statistical Centre of Iran.

45

Table E.5 Numerical distribution of employed persons aged 10 years and over by major industrial sector and sex: 1986 and 1991

Major industrial sector	1986		1991	
	Male	Female	Male	Female
Agriculture, forestry, hunting and fishing	2 931 731	259 030	3 046 283	159 147
Mining and quarrying	31 833	537	97 664	2 881
Manufacturing	1 240 543	210 787	1 710 857	302 867
Electricity, gas and water	88 793	2 251	125 757	3 243
Construction	1 196 945	9 319	1 364 117	8 320
Trade, hotel and restaurant	860 777	14 681	1 221 712	16 593
Transport, storage and communication	621 994	8 552	750 984	11 194
Finance, insurance and business	103 819	10 469	179 016	15 670
Community, social and personal services	2 635 595	414 158	2 908 674	609 223
Activities not adequately defined	314 200	45 521	460 325	102 088
All industrial sectors	10 026 230	975 305	11 865 389	1 231 226

Source: Statistical Centre of Iran.

Table E.6 Numerical distribution of employed persons aged 10 years and over by major occupational group and sex: 1986 and 1991

Major occupation group	1986		1991	
	Male	Female	Male	Female
Professional, technical and related workers	710 794	343 270	1 041 849	523 618
Administrative and managerial workers	42 895	1 534	69 884	1 533
Clerical and related workers	320 678	46 786	627 098	86 000
Sales workers	750 223	11 301	1 188 064	14 573
Service workers	423 178	32 029	562 390	37 901
Agriculture and allied workers	2 985 171	259 383	3 069 874	159 874
Production, transport, equipment operators and labourers	3 411 938	225 082	4 211 751	308 740
Workers not classifiable	1 381 353	55 920	1 094 479	98 987
All occupations	10 026 230	975 305	11 865 389	1 231 226

Source: Statistical Centre of Iran.

Table E.7 Numerical distribution of the employed population aged 10 years and over by employment status: 1986 and 1991

Employment status	1986		1991	
	Male	Female	Male	Female
Employer	327 582	13 719	386 194	9 647
Own account worker	4 211 732	178 717	5 196 554	256 498
Wage and salary worker	4 823 303	504 582	5 960 749	732 643
Private sector	*1 777 251*	*97 293*	*2 229 045*	*118 759*
Public sector	*3 046 052*	*407 289*	*3 731 704*	*613 884*
Unpaid family worker	274 120	209 873	189 593	147 440
Status not reported	389 493	68 414	132 299	84 998
All statuses	10 026 230	975 305	11 865 389	1 231 226

Source: Statistical Centre of Iran.

REFERENCES

Aghajanian, Akbar (1991), "Population change in Iran, 1966-86: A stalled demographic transition". *Population and Development Review,* vol. 17, No. 4 (December).

——— (1994), "Family planning and contraceptive use in Iran, 1967-1992" *International Family Planning Perspectives,* vol. 20, No. 2 (June).

——— (1995), "A new direction in population policy and family planning in the Islamic Republic of Iran", *Asia-Pacific Population Journal,* vol. 10, No. 1 (March).

Economist Intelligence Unit (1997), *Country Profile: Iran, 1996/97.*

Givens B.P. and C. Hirschman (1994), "Modernization and consanguineous marriage in Iran", *Journal of Marriage and the Family,* vol. 56, No. 4 (November).

Makhlouf Obermeyer, Carla (1994), "Reproductive choice in Islam: gender and state in Iran and Tunisia", *Studies in Family Planning,* vol. 25, No. 1 (January/ February).

Malek-Afzali H. (1988), "Birth and death indicators in the Islamic Republic of Iran in 1984 and 1986", *Medical Journal of the Islamic Republic of Iran,* vol. 2, No. 4.

Ministry of Health and Medical Education (1989), "KAP survey among currently married women aged 15-49 years, October 1989" (Tehran).

——— (1992), *Results of the 1992 Family Planning Survey of Iran* (Tehran).

National Committee Secretariat (1995), "National report on women in the Islamic Republic of Iran", prepared for the Fourth World Conference on Women: Equality, Development and Peace, Beijing, September 1995 (Tehran, Bureau of Women's Affairs, Office of the President of the Republic).

Payadarfar, A.A. and R. Moini (1995), "Modernization process and fertility change in pre- and post-Islamic Revolution of Iran, A cross-provincial analysis 1966-1986", *Population Research and Policy Review,* vol. 14, No. 1 (March).

Selvaratnam, S. (1988), "Population and status of women", *Asia-Pacific Population Journal,* vol. 3, No. 2 (June).

Smith, Harvey H. (1971), *Area Handbook of Iran,* 2nd ed., Foreign Area Studies (The American University. Washington, D.C).

Statistical Centre of Iran (1987), *A Statistical Reflection of the Islamic Republic of Iran: No. 4* (Tehran, Plan and Budget Ministry).

——— (1995), *A Statistical Reflection of the Islamic Republic of Iran: No. 12* (Tehran, Plan and Budget Ministry).

United Nations Children's Fund (1992), *Situation Analysis of Women and Children in Iran* (Tehran).

United Nations Educational, Scientific and Cultural Organization (1997), *Statistical Yearbook, 1996.*

United Nations Population Fund (1995), *Programme Review and Strategy Development Report: Islamic Republic of Iran,* No. 44 (New York).

United Nations (1996), *World Population Prospects: The 1996 Revision, Annexes II and III: Demographic Indicators by Major Area, Region and Country* (Population Division, Department for Economic and Social Information and Policy Analysis, New York).